Completing Your Qualitative Study

An active reference guiding you from preparation through reporting

Ayn Embar-Seddon O'Reilly
Michael K. Golebiewski
Ellen Peterson Mink

CONTENTS

ABOUT THE AUTHORS

Ayn Embar-Seddon O'Reilly

Ayn earned her undergraduate degrees in philosophy and psychology from the University of Pittsburgh. She holds a master's degree in clinical psychology from Edinboro University of Pennsylvania. She earned her Ph.D. in criminology from Indiana University of Pennsylvania after completing a qualitative case study on hospital violence for her dissertation.

She began working with doctoral level students in 2001. After seeing many students struggle with qualitative, this helpful little book was born. She has previously published a forensic science textbook and *From Concept to Completion: Writing Your Social Science Dissertation in 18 Months or Less*, also published by Helpful Little Books.

Michael K. Golebiewski

Michael has a certification in Marketing and earned his master's degree in Multimedia Technology from Duquesne University. He has taught as an adjunct professor in the fields of Multimedia and English Writing at Duquesne University and Carnegie Mellon University, respectively. He has worked for more than 20 years in professional services, honing his project management skill set and keen attention to detail. He also co-authored *From Concept to Completion: Writing Your Social Science Dissertation in 18 Months or Less*.

Ellen Peterson Mink

Ellen earned her undergraduate degree in Psychology from the State University College at Oneonta. She earned her doctorate in Counseling Psychology from the University of Buffalo after completing a quantitative dissertation on infant temperament and toddler behavior in families with alcoholic and non-alcoholic fathers. She worked for 15 years on several large-scale, federally funded, longitudinal grants focusing on child development and family dynamics in families dealing with addiction. She began mentoring doctoral students in 2009. She also co-authored *From Concept to Completion: Writing Your Social Science Dissertation in 18 Months or Less*.

PREFACE TO THE TEXT

This book is designed as an introduction to six common qualitative approaches to research. It is meant for the novice researcher or for those who are more seasoned researchers but new to qualitative. It presents the qualitative process in an easy to understand format and will give you the information you need to start you on your qualitative research journey. This text is full of advice and tips that you can use, in whole or in part to get you through your qualitative study, and backed up by activities and thought exercises, which will help move you forward. This book is meant to be a starting point in conducting qualitative research and will refer you to other qualitative resources to further your development as a qualitative researcher.

PART ONE –
AN INTRODUCTION TO QUALITATIVE

The beginning of any research study is to understand what we want to know and to create a path to obtaining that knowledge. A failure to really understand qualitative research (as with any project) will severely hamper your chances for success. From the outset it is important to understand what a qualitative study can do and when it should be undertaken. It is also important to understand the philosophical underpinnings of qualitative in general and the particular qualitative approach that you will be using in your study.

Done well, qualitative can provide depth to our understanding, leading to new knowledge and insights. Done poorly, it can become nothing more than disconnected, unscientific ramblings.

Chapter One: The Philosophical Underpinnings of Qualitative Research

Whether you are deciding to undertake a qualitative or quantitative study, that decision must be made for the right reasons. Both qualitative and quantitative are appropriate for particular types of research studies and it is important that you, as the researcher, make the correct choice. This chapter will present a comparison of qualitative and quantitative to help you decide which approach is best for your study.

The first step in making the choice to conduct a qualitative study (as with any study) is to conduct a thorough literature review of your topic. Not only is this necessary to find an appropriate gap in the literature in which to nest your study, but also because qualitative studies should only be undertaken in certain circumstances: to explore new topic areas, or new portions of more established topics. Qualitative is chosen when an exploratory study is necessary to find out *what* is out there. Once it is known what exists in the field, then quantitative studies are undertaken to allow generalizability. Quantitative often takes the concepts or themes that are derived from qualitative and attempts to determine relationships or make predictions about the way the world works.

Second, the research questions must dictate that a qualitative study should be conducted. If the research question, of example asks: "What is the most effective method of lowering recidivism rates?" a qualitative study cannot be conducted to answer the research question. Qualitative questions center around "experiences" of the individual subjects, or it can present a case study of a particular environment.

The fact that there is no qualitative literature on your topic is not an appropriate justification for a qualitative study. Some disciplines are not accepting of qualitative work, so you will find very few qualitative studies conducted. On the other hand, the literature may have developed past the point where qualitative work is appropriate.

Qualitative research and quantitative research are very different approaches to scientifically understanding what is in the world. In many ways, they are opposites. Qualitative research goes hand in hand with quantitative research in moving any discipline forward. Neither approach is fully adequate for any field. They have different purposes and if you understand each one, you will be able to choose the appropriate methodology for your study. The purpose of qualitative is explorative in nature. It seeks to tell us what "exists" in the world, but it cannot allow us to make generalizations about what we discover—that becomes the job of quantitative. The purpose of quantitative is to quantify and generalize. Quantitative methods can examine effectiveness. Certain types of quantitative research can also make predictions, which can be very valuable in letting us know how, for example, a treatment will work.

Qualitative research serves as the basis for all fields because it strives to let the researcher explore "what is there?" when it is not known what comprises the field. It is descriptive and exploratory in nature. It is also used to extend the boundaries of fields and explore new areas of fields. Qualitative research aims for depth of description, rather than generalizability—which is the goal of quantitative. We move from exploring new areas of the field with qualitative, to making generalizable statements with quantitative. When we then get to the boundary of the field again and wish to stretch into new areas—we return to qualitative. While quantitative and qualitative may often be seen as opposites, they complement each other very nicely in the development of a discipline and both types of research are required to move a discipline forward. The table below provides a brief compare-contrast of the two methodologies:

Methodological Approach	Qualitative	Quantitative
Type of reasoning	Inductive – moves from specific to general	Deductive – moves from general to specific
Number of variables	Focuses on one, and it is often referred to as a "concept"	Must have two or more
Relationship to theory	Creates and explores theory	Tests theory
Common methods	Semi- or unstructured interviews, unstructured observation, field notes	Normed, validated instruments, structured interviews, structured observation
Nature of reality	Multiple realities	One, testable reality
Role of researcher	More subjective	More objective
Type of Analyses	Mainly written	Uses numbers and statistics
Reliability, validity, credibility, confirmability	Deals with credibility and confirmability	Deals with reliability and validity

Let's discuss each of these differences in more detail.

Type of Reasoning

In science there are two types of reasoning: inductive and deductive. Both are necessary to move disciplines forward. Qualitative research is inductive. Quantitative research is deductive. Inductive research has been compared to a bottom-up approach. It moves from specific observations and moves toward the creation or exploration of theory. In a qualitative study, we examine a few subjects and move toward creating theory about how the world works. Quantitative is deductive in nature and moves from general to specific. This is why quantitative relies upon large numbers of subjects. From those large numbers, we make statements about individuals.

Number of Variables/Concepts

In qualitative research, the variable is often referred to as a concept—for example, "the experience of moving away and starting college." If this is the concept being explored in a qualitative study, then all of the data collected and analyzed will help create a full picture of the experience of moving away and starting college. Qualitative studies examine only one concept, and it seeks to explore that concept deeply.

In quantitative, there must be two or more variables. Less robust quantitative studies will examine only two variables ("parental income level and stress levels among new college students"—here we have named two variables "parental income level" and "stress levels" ("new college students" is not a variable but rather a population descriptor because all subjects are new college students), whereas more complex studies examine more than two ("stress, anxiety, and parental income level among new college students"—now there are three variables: "stress," "anxiety," and "parental income level"). Quantitative methods seek to determine how variables relate to each other, how they differ, or how predictions can be made.

Relationship to Theory

It is within each methodological approach to theory that it becomes clear how both move a discipline forward. Qualitative is used to create or explore theory. In qualitative, some researchers seek to create explanations for how they observe the world working. They create a theory to explain the world. The qualitative approach of grounded theory specifically aims at creating new theory "from the ground up." A grounded theory study is undertaken when researchers within a discipline have come to the conclusion that there is not an adequate theory to explain what they are studying—so a new one must be created. However, in most instances qualitative will be used to expand upon theory, to stretch its boundaries.

While qualitative is responsible for theory creation and expansion—it does not test theory. Theory testing is done through quantitative studies. Quantitative takes those theories created by qualitative and tests the tenants of those theories. While a theory can never be "proven" through research, it will be shown that some theories provide better explanations of the world than others do. Theories that do not obtain research support are eventually discarded.

Keep in mind, as you are reading the literature and as you are constructing your study, that not all studies have a theoretical underpinning. Many studies are atheoretical, so you may not see a theory mentioned in every journal article that you read. This is especially true in practice-based journals.

Common Methods

Qualitative and quantitative methodologists collect data in very different ways. Quantitative methods have as their main goal the quantifying (or counting) of variables and data will be in the form of numbers. Even data that is collected as words will be quantified into numbers. Qualitative methods have as their main goal the qualifying (or describing) of concepts and data will mostly be in the form of words.

Common quantitative methods include the use of measures, instruments, forced-choice surveys, structured interviews, and structured observation. All of these are an attempt to quantify the object under study—whether that is depression or leadership styles, or intelligence.

Qualitative methods have as their goal providing rich details about the subject. They aim at depth. The most common qualitative method is the semi-structured interview. Most researchers collect their qualitative data in a face-to face interview format. Other common methods include field notes, observations, diaries, newspapers, and photographs.

Nature of Reality

Philosophically speaking, qualitative and quantitative methodologists view the world in very different ways. Quantitative researchers hold a positivist worldview. There is one, objective, measurable reality that exists outside of the individual who is doing the observing or measuring. The researcher seeks to measure this objective world. Because there is one reality that exists outside of the individual, it is possible to create instruments to measure that reality.

Qualitative researchers hold a social constructivist worldview. In social constructivism, the subjects construct their reality—which doesn't exist outside of the individuals who perceive or experience it. In qualitative, there are multiple realities and each individual has his or her own reality. Because reality is different for each subject, the researcher must listen to how the subject describes his or her own reality to understand the object of the research.

Role of Researcher

Qualitative researchers function differently than quantitative researchers and how they see themselves within the research is also very different. In any quantitative study, the researcher strives to be as objective as possible. You can see how this fits in with their view of the nature of reality—there is one objective reality and the researcher who investigates and tries to discover that reality is also objective in the research process.

Perhaps the best example of this is the double-blind study commonly used to investigate drug and other medical interventions. In a double-blind study, not only do the subjects not know if they are receiving the active drug or a placebo (they are "blind") but also, the person administering the intervention is blind to who is in the experimental group and who is in the control group. The double-blind design is used to guard against both placebo effect and experimenter bias.

In a qualitative study, the researcher is more subjective. You will often hear phrases such as: "the researcher as instrument" used in qualitative, this means that when you conduct qualitative research, there is far more subjectivity involved in the study. How you collect the data, organize the data, and analyze the data is very much done through you. Since much qualitative data is gathered through the interview process—how the researcher conducts the interview, the researcher's voice, gender, manner of dress, age, race, and so forth can all impact how subjects react to both the researcher and the questions asked during the interview. Everything in the study is filtered through the lens of who you are as a person and as a researcher. This does not mean that you are wholly subjective, that there is no scientific objectivity involved, or that you are just writing about yourself in a solipsistic manner. In order for you to be subjective, yet still maintain some research objectivity, special training must be undertaken and special design features are put into place in a qualitative study. Training for conducting an interview or observations is necessary and much practice is necessary. Design features like "member-checking" and "triangulation" are also often put into place.

Type of Analysis

Qualitative analysis is mostly written, while quantitative uses numbers and statistics. In a typical qualitative study, you will be describing the data with words. You may be describing themes or presenting a narrative. Qualitative methodologists are not concerned with averages or even how many of your subjects (sometimes referred to as co-researchers in a qualitative study) mentioned a particular theme. In fact, in a qualitative study a theme that is mentioned by one individual may be just as important as a theme mentioned by all of the subjects.

In quantitative, of course, the researcher is relying on numbers to communicate to the reader. Quantitative methodologists will present descriptive statistics like averages and modes as a matter of course. They will also present statistics designed to let the reader know how variables relate to each other or to make predictions. Quantitative studies must have large numbers of subjects (although some statistics can be run with 50 subjects—most studies have over 100 and some have thousands). In a quantitative study, a response that is only given by one subject or only a few may be considered to be an "outlier." Quantitative is very much concerned with how *most* of the subjects respond and quantitative always seeks to make generalizations from the research.

Reliability, Validity, Confirmability, Credibility

In quantitative research we speak of validity and reliability in reference to instrumentation and measurement. Validity tells us whether or not an instrument measures what it purports to measure. Reliability, on the other hand, refers to how consistently an instrument measures what it purports to measure. Well-constructed instruments are both valid and reliable. For example, the Beck Depression Inventory (Beck, Steer, & Brown,1996). is an excellent instrument that can be used to measure depression, as it has strong psychometric properties. So when an instrument is both valid and reliable it measures what it purports to measure and it will do so time after time. Choosing such measures for research increases the faith quantitative researchers have in their results and strengthens their ability to accurately generalize findings.

The terms of validity and reliability are generally not used in qualitative research, because qualitative research does not measure the world in the same way quantitative research does. However it is important that qualitative research be an adequate representation and interpretation of the world. To this end, the terms confirmability, credibility, transferability, and dependability are used to refer to how well qualitative research "gets at" the real world (Guba, 1981; Lincoln, & Guba, 2007).

Confirmability refers to whether or not the researcher has attempted to eliminate his or her own biases in the research. This is an especial challenge in qualitative, where the researcher is, in fact, an instrument. Qualitative researchers openly acknowledge that all research and all researchers have biases. As researchers we are biased in the research we choose to pursue, the methodological approach we take to that research, the research questions we compose, the methods we choose to answer those research questions, and the interview questions we write. The qualitative researcher will attempt to limit biases by situating the study within the larger literature and by choosing tried-and-true methods that are appropriate for answering the research questions that have been posed. Biases are also removed from the research by having interview questions field tested (reviewed by other experts) prior to use and through researcher triangulation—where multiple researchers review all aspects of the study.

Credibility is concerned with how the results from the study are representative of the external world. This begins with the literature review leading up to the study. The current research project should fit in with previous research and this academic grounding lends credibility to the study. Credibility can also be heightened through the various forms of triangulation. Through triangulation of methods, multiple types of data are collected to create a fuller picture of the object of the study. Through researcher triangulation, credibility is enhanced by having more than one researcher review the data. Member-checking can be used to allow subjects to review their own statements. This provides an opportunity for them to clarify or add to what they have previously said. The researcher may also need to build in a method for double-checking the veracity of the subjects' statements, for example, reviewing other existing accounts of what happened, from a newspaper or from police reports. This is especially important for situations where the subjects may misremember what has happened (if considerable time has passed) or may have impetus to not be entirely truthful (if the object of the interview deals with potentially embarrassing behavior). The researcher can also enhance credibility by using well-developed and accepted qualitative methods.

Transferability is concerned with how the results of the current study are representative of other similar studies. This is similar to generalizability in quantitative—however it does not utilize the large numbers that generalizability in quantitative requires. The results from any qualitative study should inform the literature. Finally, dependability requires that the researcher fully describe the study design and utilize appropriate qualitative methods.

Drawbacks of Qualitative

Qualitative studies take a considerable investment of time, money, training and writing ability. Qualitative studies are time consuming because most of them rely upon long, semi-structured interviews as their main method of data collection. These interviews may last anywhere from 20 minutes to more than an hour. In some cases, there may be multiple interviews of the same participant. The transcription of all of this data takes time—as does the analysis. Subject recruitment can be time-consuming—even when you are dealing with only a handful of subjects.

Qualitative studies can be very expensive. If you are conducting a qualitative study for your dissertation, you will still be paying tuition during your study—and in some cases, good qualitative studies can take years to complete, for example, in an ethnographic study it is not uncommon for the researcher to spend six months or more just becoming acquainted with the field. If you are conducting face-to-face interviews, you may have travel expenses. It will cost money to have your interviews transcribed—unless you do the transcription yourself. If you utilize qualitative software to help you organize your data, this will be an added expense in your study.

While both quantitative and qualitative research require training, because the researcher serves as an instrument in the qualitative study and normed, validated instruments cannot be relied upon like they can in quantitative, the researcher must devote considerable time and effort to training. You will require training in the methods that you will be utilizing in your study. You will require training in data analysis.

Unlike quantitative studies, which are all about the statistics and the numbers, qualitative studies rely upon the writing and your ability to write. Qualitative is a narrative. You need to be able to tell the story of your subjects to your reader and you need to tell in in a way that is meaningful to your discipline. This is not an easy task. Qualitative writing must be engaging writing.

We have heard students mention the following reasons why they wanted to do a qualitative study: "I'm a people person," "I'm not a math person," "It's easier than quantitative." In actuality, these are never good reasons for undertaking the commitment of a qualitative study. While there is generally more interaction with people in the course of a qualitative study, because you will often be conducting interviews or doing field observations, just being a "people person" really isn't enough to be able to conduct a solid qualitative study.

Some students may gravitate to qualitative because it does not require performing any statistics. While this is true, it has been our experience that statistics are very cut-and-dry, and statistical procedures can be taught by taking a course or two, yet appropriate qualitative procedures are very difficult to teach and require many hours of practice. While it is difficult to conduct a good qualitative interview it is even more difficult to analyze hours and hours of qualitative interviews and make sense of all that data.

It's usually the absence of statistics that makes qualitative seem easier—in actuality this makes it more difficult. Qualitative analysis, unlike statistical analysis is not clear-cut. Much of qualitative analysis is open to considerable interpretation—and therein lays the difficulty. It's so open-ended. There is not one correct analysis. It takes considerable time to learn about and understand qualitative data collection, qualitative data analysis, and how to do a good qualitative write-up. It is far easier to learn statistics than it is to conduct a quantitative study.

We do not say all of this to discourage you from qualitative—quite the contrary. We love qualitative and we want you to love it too, but qualitative studies represent considerable commitment in terms of time, energy, and money and the qualitative path is one that should only be chosen knowingly.

Strengths of Qualitative

There are many strengths of qualitative research: including more involvement of the researcher with the subjects, the ability to explore the topic area in greater depth, the opportunity to write more, and the flexibility that qualitative methods allows. It takes considerable skill to conduct a good qualitative interview, through qualitative interviewing the researcher is more involved with his or her subjects—so much so that some qualitative researchers refer to their subjects as "co-researchers"—acknowledging how important their role is in the research. For any researcher that feels that conducting research should be done as a relationship, qualitative may be a good fit.

Others find the depth and detail of qualitative to be very attractive. While quantitative allows us to make generalizations—it only allows us to look at a narrow piece of the world— qualitative provides us with the opportunity to explore the experience of individuals in our study in considerable depth. This depth better allows the researcher to explore what it is like to be human and interact with other humans in the world—this richness of the human experience is often noted to be lacking in much quantitative research.

Qualitative research is ideal for any researcher that enjoys writing and helping others to tell the story of their experiences. Although the writing task associated with qualitative might be considered a burden by some—for those who truly love writing, it can be ideal. Through the written word, the researcher is better able to convey the fullness of the human experience—something not available in the numbers used in quantitative.

Quantitative research is very rigid in what it will allow the researcher to do during the research process. Once a quantitative research study is designed, it should not be altered. When quantitative instruments are used in any research study, they must be administered in the same fashion to each subject. Qualitative research, on the other hand, allows great flexibility. In some forms of qualitative, the research is begun without a theoretical underpinning, or without research questions and hypotheses. During qualitative interviewing, researchers do not have to ask the subjects all questions in the same way or even in the same order. The researcher is allowed to explore topics that the subject brings up during the interview that were not anticipated. If a tiered interview process is used, the interview questions can even be changed during the research.

What Cannot Be Done With Qualitative

There are limitations as to what qualitative methods can accomplish; in order for your research to have merit, you must stay within these boundaries. Qualitative methods cannot be used to measure effectiveness, link variables, establish cause and effect, or create generalizations. All of this can only be done through various types of quantitative studies.

It is not possible to evaluate the effectiveness of a program or intervention through qualitative research—although you can talk to people about their experiences in an effective program—however, that word "effective" is quite a sticking point. You need to define for your research—"what does effective mean?" An effective math tutoring program for children might be a program that allows a child to perform better on a standardized test after completion of the program—or advance one grade level. An effective program for juvenile offenders would lower the recidivism rate for those juveniles. A common error made by novice qualitative researchers—is attempting to examine effectiveness through perceptions or feelings. Effectiveness however is not based upon how we feel or perceive a program and asking how individuals "feel" about effectiveness or their "experiences of effective training" has little value. Take the example of the original D.A.R.E. program. It was very popular and received considerable funding and support. However, it did not lower drug use level among its graduates—even though many of the graduates had high praise for the program (Gottfredson, 1998).

Qualitative can never link variables. In fact, a hallmark of qualitative is that it examines only one concept. If you want to know how X relates to Y (for example how type of graduate program relates to later salary) you cannot answer this research question with qualitative research. You could examine "women's experiences in an online graduate program" but that is only one variable (concept). You would not attempt to examine how their experiences related to their salary—that can only be done through quantitative.

It is not possible, in any way, to establish cause and effect with qualitative. It is actually very difficult to establish cause and effect in social science research. In the physical sciences, cause and effect is established through the use of experiments and control over variables involved in the experiment.

Finally, you cannot generalize from qualitative research beyond your subjects. In fact, the nature of qualitative is that it does not yield to generalizations. The sample size in qualitative is very small—sometimes you will have fewer than ten subjects. Making generalizations requires a large sample size. Generalizations can only be made through quantitative and the use of statistical analysis.

Definition of Terms

This book uses many technical terms that are used in discussing qualitative research. These are generally defined during the first instance of their use, but this section is provided as a single location resource to list many of the most important terms used throughout this book.

Action Research – a type of research that focuses on solving a problem – often in a workplace. It may range from only making recommendations for change to actually implementing an intervention.

Approach or Qualitative Approach – how your research is set up, your design (for example: case study, phenomenology)

Autoethnography – an ethnographic study where the researcher is the subject of the research.

Belmont Report – a report created by the National Commission for the Protection of Human Subjects of Biomedical and Behavioral Research that is used as one of the guides for the ethical conducting of research.

Bracketing – in phenomenology this is the process of the researcher setting aside his or her own judgment; also referred to as epoché or phenomenological reduction.

Case Study – a qualitative design that looks at a bounded system (a system that has clear boundaries like a workplace or a classroom) and always uses triangulation.

Confirmability – to add strength to a qualitative study the researcher attempts to eliminate his/her own biases.

Constructivism (Social Constructivism) – the theoretical underpinning for qualitative research, which holds that there are multiple realities and it is the subjects view of the world that creates reality.

Concept – some qualitative researchers use this term to refer to a qualitative "variable." While quantitative always explores two or more variables, qualitative explores one concept within a study.

Credibility – in a qualitative study, this is an indication of how representative the results are of other similar studies.

Critical Research – research undertaken that aligns with critical theory and is generally action oriented.

Critical Theory – a theory based in Marxist Theory that has at its core the questioning of power differentials.

Dependability – dependability requires that the researcher fully describe the study design and utilize appropriate qualitative methods.

Design – how your research is set up, also referred to as an approach or qualitative approach or methodological approach.

Epoché – in phenomenology this is the process of the researcher setting aside his or her own judgment; also referred to as bracketing or phenomenological reduction.

Ethnography – a qualitative design that arose from the field of anthropology, which looks at a culture, subculture, or microculture.

Gatekeeper – in research, an individual who can be seen as having control over access to a research setting or subjects within that setting.

Grounded Theory – a qualitative design that has as its goal to create new theory. This can be contrasted with quantitative designs, which often are utilized to test existing theory.

Guiding Interview Questions – the list of questions that guide a qualitative interview, sometimes also referred to as an interview schedule or guiding interview questions.

Human Subjects Research – most of our research in the social sciences involves human subjects. In qualitative, because we almost always directly interact with our subjects, there can be many more ethical issues as compared to quantitative.

IRB (Institutional Review Board) – a panel that reviews all research at an institution for the purpose of the protection of human subjects; these panels may—depending upon the type of institution—also review other types of studies as well, such as clinical studies or animal research. There must be an IRB at any school that conducts research. You can also commonly find IRBs at hospitals. There are also private IRBs that review the research of independent researchers who are not affiliated with a university or hospital that has an IRB.

IRB Review – the review conducted by the IRB. You must receive approval for your research from your university's IRB before you can collect data.

Exempt IRB Review – this is the briefest of IRB reviews and does not require the full IRB committee to meet and review the proposal. Research that falls under this type of review is of minimal risk to subjects.

Expedited IRB Review – this review is not as short as the exempt review but not nearly as lengthy as the full review. The research must be minimal risk and not involve a vulnerable population.

Full IRB Review – this is the longest and most exacting IRB review. It requires that the full IRB committee sit and review the proposal. It may also require that special reviewers sit and review the proposal if protected populations are involved in the research, for example individuals under the control of the criminal justice system or those with disabilities.

Informant – in ethnography this is an individual who is chosen because of his or her knowledge and place in the community under study.

Instrument – a tool that is used for measurement in research, such as a survey or questionnaire. In some instances, you will see an interview schedule referred to as an instrument, but the term instrument is more commonly used in quantitative research. Qualitative research will often speak of "the researcher as instrument" to refer to the intimate involvement of the researcher in the research.

Interview Guide – a name for the list of questions that subjects are asked, can also be referred to as an interview schedule, or guiding interview questions.

Interview Schedule – the list of questions used in an interview. This is often seen as more structured than guiding interview questions or an interview guide—but the terms are sometimes used interchangeably.

Methodology and Method – while these terms have different meanings, they are often used interchangeably. Technically, "methodology" is the study of method. "Method" refers to the particular ways in which a study is conducted. The third chapter of the dissertation is entitled either "Methodology" or "Method," but it is the chapter that provides the specific directions for how your study will be (in the case of the proposal) or was (in the case of the dissertation) carried out.

Methodological approach – within the broad methodologies of quantitative and qualitative research there are the approaches that are used to guide a study.

Narrative approach – a qualitative approach that is grounded in the story of the subject.

Phenomenological reduction – in phenomenology this is the process of the researcher setting aside his or her own judgment; also referred to as epoché or bracketing.

Phenomenology – a qualitative approach that looks at a phenomenon. These studies often seek to get at the "lived experiences" of the subjects.

Positivism – the theoretical underpinning for quantitative research, which holds that reality is discernible through empirical studies.

Qualitative Research – a research approach that generally relies upon verbal data from only a few subjects and explores those subjects in depth.

Qualitative Software Packages – these are computer packages that are used to help organize qualitative data; but they do not perform analyses. Common software packages include NVivo, Atlas ti, and QDAP among others.

Quantitative Research – a research approach based in positivism that relies upon the collection of large amounts of numerical data and the use of statistics.

Reliability – in a quantitative study, how consistently an instrument measures what it purports to measure.

Scientific Merit – this is a determination of whether a study advances the scientific knowledge base and is solidly constructed. IRBs consider the scientific merit of a study prior to approval in addition to ethical issues.

Sociogram – A diagram that outlines the relationships among a group of people, and is often used in ethnography.

Theory – a set of interrelated statements that scientifically explains a phenomenon.

Transferability – refers to how representative the results of a qualitative study are of other similar studies.

Triangulation – a method of verifying results of qualitative research.

Triangulation of Data or Methods – the collecting of multiple types of data to "get at" one particular phenomena—one of the hallmarks of the case study.

Researcher Triangulation – having more than one researcher work with the data to strengthen statements made about the research.

Theory Triangulation – where multiple theories are used to interpret the data.

Validity – in a quantitative study, refers to whether or not an instrument measures what it purports to measure.

Vulnerable Population – a vulnerable population in research is a group in which there is a greater potential for harm from research because of characteristics of those individuals. Children are considered a vulnerable population because they lack the capacity to give informed consent. Prisoners are also a vulnerable population because they do not have the same ability as other subjects to decline participation in research. Anyone with diminished mental capacity is considered vulnerable because they may lack the understanding required to consent to research.

Qualitative Research Preparation

Research preparation is key for conducting any good qualitative study, yet there are few graduate programs that boast extensive qualitative courses. The best qualitative training consists not only of courses that teach qualitative, but also extensive reading in qualitative and working in qualitative research, ideally under a faculty member who has extensive experience with qualitative. Ideally, prior to conducting your own qualitative study, you will spend years being trained in qualitative, first helping a faculty member with their qualitative studies, including all aspects of a qualitative study. This will include designing a study, writing up a study, presenting a study, and then moving on into more autonomous roles, choosing an area to research and conduct your own studies. But circumstances are rarely ideal, and when they aren't you need to take it upon yourself to obtain the appropriate training to conduct your qualitative study.

Take the following "Qualitative Research Preparedness Questionnaire" and see where your qualitative strengths and weaknesses lie:

Qualitative Research Preparedness Questionnaire

Working with a Faculty Member		
Worked under a research faculty member as an undergraduate	Yes	No
Worked under a research faculty member at the graduate level	Yes	No
There are opportunities at my current school to work under a research faculty member doing qualitative research	Yes	No
Taking Qualitative Courses		
Have taken a course in qualitative research	Yes	No
Have taken more than one course in qualitative research	Yes	No
There are opportunities for me to take qualitative research courses	Yes	No

Publishing and Presenting, Teaching		
Have taught or tutored qualitative research methods	Yes	No
There are opportunities for me to teach qualitative research Methods	Yes	No
Was actively involved in publishing/presenting research at the undergraduate level	Yes	No
Was actively involved in publishing/presenting research at the graduate level	Yes	No
There are opportunities for me to currently publish and present	Yes	No
Attending Conferences and Reading Qualitative		
Have read extensively on qualitative research	Yes	No
Subscribe to one or more qualitative journals	Yes	No
Have attended one or more qualitative conferences	Yes	No
There are opportunities for me to attend qualitative conferences	Yes	No

If you answered with many "yes" responses, you are probably well prepared for conducting a qualitative study. If you answered with many "no" responses, this helps you know where some of your weaknesses lie. Also, notice that the questionnaire is broken down into four areas—take note what areas could benefit from more attention. If you are taking this Research Preparedness Questionnaire early in your academic career, you may want to arrange courses or learning opportunities to address any weaknesses that this has revealed. Lets discuss these areas in a bit more depth.

Working under a research faculty member

The best preparation for any activity is to be guided by someone else who is an expert in that activity. So, one of the best preparations for conducting your own qualitative research is to work extensively under another person who is conducting qualitative research. At the very minimum, working under a faculty member who is doing qualitative research will expose you to the process of research. You learn not only by watching more seasoned members of the research team doing their jobs, but also by performing progressively more responsible research tasks on your own. You may begin by performing entry-level research jobs like scheduling interviews, and then move into more and more responsibility like conducting interviews. You may even be lucky enough to be mentored by a faculty member. Having a mentoring relationship can provide many benefits to you in your own research and in your career.

Have taken one or more courses in qualitative research

Along with being a member of a research team and working under a faculty member who conducts qualitative studies, taking formal courses in qualitative research is excellent preparation for conducting your own study. Through coursework in the area of qualitative methods, you will be exposed to the theoretical underpinnings of the qualitative approach and will study a variety of qualitative approaches in depth. In a classroom environment, you can have your questions answered by an expert. Some courses may even have you assemble a potential study.

Have taught qualitative research methods

Nothing prepares you quite as well for conducting qualitative research as having taught qualitative methodology to either undergraduates or graduate students. This allows you to take the knowledge you have acquired and transmit it to others. If you have the opportunity to teach a class, we would suggest that you take it. The preparation that you will do for teaching alone will really help you solidify what you know about qualitative. Responding to the questions of your students will allow you to strengthen your understanding of areas that may have been previously weak.

Involved in publishing/presenting qualitative research

Although we would not recommend it as a beginning step in your study of qualitative, certainly, at some point, you will want to publish and/or present your qualitative research. Disciplines only move forward when research is shared. It can be very daunting at first, but the very act of preparing your research for possible publication or for a presentation forces you to see your research in a different way and to learn more about qualitative. You may know all about your research—but for publications and presentations, you must be able to present your qualitative research clearly to others so that they can use the knowledge that you have produced in their own research and you must be able to respond to questions about your study.

You should also consider publishing and presenting for a non-academic, professional audience. Much of the research that is conducted is only shared with other academicians— when much of it has application in the professional, practice sphere. For many of our disciplines, a significant portion of that discipline is practice and our research should be shared with those professionals who are out in the field as well. Publishing and presenting for a professional audience means translating your research from the academic sphere into the professional sphere; while an academic audience may be concerned with theory creation, a professional audience is concerned with how your research will impact their daily work lives. The greatest benefit of sharing your work with a professional audience is that it will allow your research to be applied in the field immediately through these professionals.

Have attended one or more qualitative conferences

While conferences that focus on qualitative methodology do not teach you qualitative methodology, they are an excellent way to enhance your knowledge of qualitative methods, to get-together with other qualitative researchers and compare perspectives on qualitative. Qualitative research is very much a developing approach, with methods that are changing and growing. Attending conferences is one step on the way to presenting at these same conferences. The point is to go, expose yourself to qualitative, take notes, learn, and get the feel for what conferences are all about.

Have read extensively on qualitative research

While it is not a good idea to attempt to teach yourself qualitative from books and journal articles alone, these can be a great supplement to what you have learned in classes or under the direction of another qualitative researcher. Even if you are not interested in learning more about qualitative in general, you will need to read extensively on qualitative to make an informed choice about the qualitative methodology for your study. When you begin your reading you will start with more general qualitative texts that discuss a variety of qualitative approaches side-by-side (for example, Berg, 2009). Once you have narrowed down your choice of approaches, you will want to read more extensively about one or two of the qualitative approaches until you make a decision (for example, the works of Clark Moustakas if you are interested in phenomenology and the works of Robert Stake if you are interested in case study). At that point, you will want to read extensively on your chosen approach, including both books and journals. As a general guideline, we would recommend having at least 15-25 good methodological references for any qualitative study—more if you are working on a dissertation.

Your qualitative reading also should not stop with the completion of your dissertation or first qualitative study. You should continue to read extensively on qualitative throughout your career if you plan on conducting more than one qualitative study. Anyone who is interested in teaching qualitative should also be actively reading all the time.

Subscribe to one or more qualitative journals

As part of your reading, you will want to read certain qualitative journals (please see the list included at the end of the text). You will want to choose journals within your discipline and also that focus on the qualitative approach that you are utilizing. Once you have decided to pursue a qualitative approach, you will want to begin subscribing to one or more qualitative journals through your university library. You may also want to read articles published by particular qualitative researchers. Through author and journal notification, your school's library can send you e-mail notifications when your favorite qualitative journal is published or when a particular author publishes. This makes your life easy—all you need to do is read!

The Research Log

In our previous book "From Concept to Completion: Writing Your Social Science Dissertation in 18 Months or Less," we discussed using the research log in the context of the dissertation, but it is a tool that is helpful during any research endeavor, so we have included it here.

The research log can help you organize the books and articles that you collect for your literature review and make them more useful to you in your research and writing. I (O'Reilly) used the paper version of the research log when I was working on my dissertation—but you may find a digital version more amenable to your work.

The research log should include all of the information that you need for your references. It will also include a brief summary of each article or book. It's a good idea to use some sort of spreadsheet program to create your log and use at least the following columns: author, date published, title, journal name if it is an article, theory, methods, design, findings, and notes.

Author	Date Published	Title	Journal name	Theories used	Method used	Design used	Major findings	Notes

Of course, this is just an example—work with it for a while and you can add the columns that you need to best assist you in tracking your research. This will help you conduct your literature review and it will help you refine your methodology. When you are reading so much it can be difficult to keep track of it all—the research log provides a shorthand way of being able to see all of the important parts of the literature that you have reviewed.

General Qualitative References

Beck, A. T., Steer, R. A., & Brown, G. K. (1996). Manual for the Beck Depression Inventory-II. San Antonio, TX: Psychological Corporation.

Gottfredson, D. C. (1998). School-based Crime Prevention. In L. W. Sherman, D. Gottfredson, D. MacKinsey, J. Eck, P. Reuter & S. Bushway (Eds.),Preventing Crime: What works, what doesn't, what's promising. Washington D.C.: U.S. Department of Justice

Guba, E. G. (1981). Criteria for assessing the trustworthiness of naturalistic inquiries, *Educational Communication and Technology Journal, 29*, 75–91.

Lincoln, Y. S., & Guba, E. G. (2007). Judging interpretations: But is it rigorous? Trustworthiness and authenticity in naturalistic evaluation. *New Directions for Evaluation, 114*, 11–25.

PART TWO:
COMMON QUALITATIVE APPROACHES

It can be difficult to create a definitive list of qualitative approaches and designs since a case could be made that some of the designs that we discuss here overlap or might more correctly be considered a philosophical approach to research rather than just a design. For our purposes, however, the qualitative designs are: case study, phenomenology, generic qualitative, ethnography, grounded theory, and narrative. If you have a basic understanding of these six designs you have a good start in your understanding of qualitative design. We will also discuss action research and critical research. Action research has as its goal addressing a problem. Critical research has as its goal examining power structures and differentials. Both action research and critical research are often qualitative in nature.

At the end of each of the chapters in this second part of the text you will find a data analysis example. Each example takes the same study but adapts it to the qualitative approach in that chapter. There are many ways to construct any study, but whatever qualitative approach is chosen will change the nature of the study.

Qualitative Methodology Worksheet

After you have read the chapters in part two, fill out the worksheet below detailing your qualitative methodology. The goal is for you to be able to fully respond to all of the questions on this worksheet. Any question that is difficult to answer should be examined in greater depth. Go back to that chapter in this section, or do outside reading.

My qualitative design is:_____

_____

This design is appropriate because:_____

_____

The strengths of my design are:_____

_____

_____

_____

The weaknesses of my design are:_____

_____

_____

_____

This design should not be changed because:_____

_____

_____

_____

My research questions are *(keep in mind most qualitative has only one or two)* research questions:___

_____

_____

The concept in each of my research questions is:_____

_____

_____

These are the main methodological references I will be using to inform my study *(this is just a starting point)*:_____

_____

_____

_____

_____

_____

I will use the following method(s) to collect data *(remember, case study requires three)*:_____

_____

_____

_____

_____

My subjects will be (be specific!):_____

_____

These are the steps I will take to recruit my subjects:_____

_____

_____

_____

_____

These are the steps in my data collection *(this should read almost like a cookbook):*_____

_____

_____

_____

_____

_____

_____

These are the steps in my data analysis *(remember, you will be following the steps set forth by a well-known methodologist in whatever qualitative approach you have chosen):*_____

_____

_____

_____

_____

_____

_____

These are the ethical considerations related to my study *(you will want to return to this after you have read* Ethical Issues and the Institutional Review Board*):*_____

_____

_____

_____

_____

_____

Chapter Two: Case Study

The case study is probably the most frequently utilized qualitative design. It is common not only in the social sciences but in educational research and medicine as well, as such, in the literature you will find many different permutations of case study discussed, from case studies that involve only a single individual to case studies that can involve hundreds, from qualitative case studies to mixed-method case studies to quantitative case studies. Keep this in mind as you explore the methodological case study literature beyond this text and don't assume that the words "case study" will always refer to the same methodological approach.

There are two hallmarks to the case study: it represents a bounded system and triangulation within the case study. Any case study must examine a "bounded system," also referred to as a unit. It can be spatially bound, like a workplace or a school setting (or even a person), or it can be event-bound, like "Hurricane Katrina survivors," or an activity, like "the intake of new inmates into a minimum security prison." But the fact that it is intrinsically bounded allows both researcher and reader to clearly know where that case begins and ends. The boundaries of any case study should be very clear because these boundaries let you know what should be included in your case study and what should be excluded. Unlike other qualitative approaches, such as phenomenology or grounded theory, which could entail almost limitless data collection, the case study is clearly finite. The researcher, even a novice researcher knows when to stop collecting data, knows what does not fit within the research because the boundaries of the case are clear and if those boundaries are not clear—then the researcher does not have a case study. If you are interested in perceptions of violence in hospital emergency departments, then you know that your data will focus on emergency departments and not the ICU or the pediatric department. The work environment of the emergency department bounds the study.

The second hallmark of the case study is the triangulation of data—or the collection of multiple data types. Triangulation can be used in any qualitative research study to strengthen the credibility of your research through cross-verification, but triangulation is required in a case study. The different types of data are used to create a more complete picture of the subject matter by examining it from different vantage points. Triangulation is generally achieved through the use of three different methods of data collection (for example, long, semi-structured interviews, document review, and observations). Triangulation can also be achieved within one method of data collection (for example, when interviews are conducted with multiple stakeholders in the study—doctors, nurses and medical social workers). This can be helpful when it is difficult to collect three different types of data. The purpose of triangulation is to strengthen the study through the multiple vantage points, which increases the credibility of the research study.

The two hallmarks of the case study are also the greatest challenges to conducting a case study. If the object that you wish to study is not a bounded system, if the boundaries are not clearly delineated, then it can be difficult to force it into a case study design. The other major challenge, of course, is to actually come up with three different types of data that can be collected and that make sense as points of data collection. We have known many students to abandon a case study design because of this sticking point. If it is not possible to conduct observations in a naturalistic setting or utilize field notes, and if it doesn't make sense to interview three different types of subjects, the case study design may not be an option for your study.

Another challenge that presents itself in case study research is a matter of terminology. Many disciplines use the word "case," and even within a discipline the term may be used in a variety of ways. We use the word "case" to mean an example. We use the phrase "case history," to refer to the medical background of a patient. We use the word "case" to refer to a criminal investigation or a type of law. So it is important that when we utilize the term "case study," we are using it appropriately for research and using it in another way.

Perhaps the key benefit to the case study methodology lies in its flexibility. While there is some restrictiveness to a case study because it must focus on a bounded system and it can be challenging to choose three different and appropriate types of data to collect, case study also has great flexibility, especially in terms of data collection.

Within a case study, as one of your types of data, you might choose to collect quantitative data, or you might choose to collect a type of data that could not stand on its own in a study. For example, if a student was interested in looking at "Challenges African American women face in healthcare leadership," a leadership styles survey could be administered to the subjects and the information gleaned from the survey could be used as a talking point within the interview. Quantitative data could also be collected from a much larger sample and incorporated within the study, for example, by administering the survey to 150 African American women in healthcare leadership positions. This allows you to utilize quantitative data without having to move into a mixed-methods study—although, this is often referred to as a mixed-methods case study!

The case study design can also allow you to collect a type of data that would not be strong enough to stand on its own, for example, descriptive statistics on a particular population. So while it is interesting to know the percentage of African American women who are in healthcare leadership positions in the country and the length of time they have been in those positions—these data points are not very robust, but they could be incorporated into a case study to help create a fuller picture of what is being studied.

Types of Case Study

There are a variety of typologies of case studies that appear in the literature. Stake's (1995) typology makes the distinction between the *intrinsic, instrumental,* and *collective* case studies. Yin (2003) organizes case studies as exploratory, explanatory, and descriptive. Distinctions can be made based upon the methods used within the case study; such as the qualitative case study, quantitative case study, and mixed-methods case study. Distinctions can also be made based upon the structure of the case study; such as a longitudinal case study—which looks at a case over time and a comparative case study, which compares two (or more) cases. You will notice as we discuss these different types of case studies that there is overlap among the types—so an "intrinsic case study" could also be an "exploratory case study," for example, or the intrinsic case study could be conducted over time and would also be considered a longitudinal case study.

Regardless of which type of case study you choose for your research you must thoroughly describe it in the methods section of your write-up. Allow the methodological literature to guide you through your case study because everything that you need to know about case study design, data collection, data analysis, and case study write-up exists within the methodological literature.

The intrinsic case study (Stake, 1995) has as its object of interest that particular case, for example, if we wanted to find out why a social service agency was not running efficiently. A case study could be constructed to examine that work environment alone. What we would learn would not help us understand other work environments and it would not help us to build theory—it would just help us understand that one case. This type of case study can be very beneficial for individuals engaged in action research—where the point of the research is to address a particular problem.

Individuals within the field often undertake intrinsic case studies and these case studies tend to be atheoretical (lack of the use of theory as the underpinning of research) in orientation. Because the goal of the study is generally to understand (and assist) that work environment there is little thought paid to expanding theory or expanding the academic literature. Most of these are unpublished and are conducted solely to assist that particular work environment. This is not to state that the intrinsic case study is not valuable. It can be valuable to that workplace and it can be valuable as a starting point for a long-range examination of a broader problem.

The instrumental case study, in contrast to the intrinsic case study, has as its object of interest a broader view of other instances like that case (Stake, 1995). For example, if we were interested in finding out why social service agencies *in general* are run inefficiently, we could study an agency that is not running efficiently, but our goal is to learn something in general about the inefficiency of social service agencies.

However, the most significant downside to the instrumental case study is that it is attempting to generalize from a particular instance to other instances—we are taking the one case and attempting to learn something about those sorts of cases in general. As we know, generalizability is a sticking point within qualitative. The drawbacks to the instrumental case study can be addressed through the collective case study.

The collective case study combines multiple instrumental cases into one study (Stake, 1995). It has as its goal learning about other instances like the cases you have selected. Combining multiple case studies into one study strengthens our ability to make statements about that particular type of case.

Yin's (2003) exploratory case study has data collection occurring before choice of theory and before creation of the research questions. This would be the most basic type of case study, asking what "exists" in the world. It is ideal for exploration in a new area of the discipline where little is known. The researcher is seeking to "get the lay of the land."

The explanatory case study attempts to answer a "how" or "why" question. It seeks to explain the case under study. Yin states that the explanatory design should be used to link an event with it effects and can be used to investigate causality—however, we would caution against attempting to make causal statements based solely upon qualitative, case study research not only because causality is difficult to get at with qualitative research but because causal statements are difficult to make in many types of studies within the social sciences. It is better to view the explanatory case study as a beginning attempt to explain what is happening in a particular case. After the explanatory case study is completed, you can then move forward with quantitative research that might allow you to examine cause.

The descriptive case study, as its name suggests describes the case that is under study. Unlike the exploratory case study, the descriptive case study will utilize a theory to guide it. It seeks to describe events in the context in which they occur.

There has also been a distinction made among case studies by the methods that are utilized within it. The qualitative case study is comprised wholly of qualitative methods. The quantitative case study is comprised wholly of quantitative methods. The mixed-methods case study is comprised of a mixture of qualitative and quantitative methods.

Case Study Data Analysis Example

How case study data is analyzed, naturally, depends upon which types of data were collected. Please read the "Qualitative Methods" chapter for a more complete discussion of data analysis for each method. The researcher must have a clear plan for data collection and data analysis for each type of data. The methods of data collection will be both considered separately and together within the study. Stake (1995) speaks of "individual instances" and "aggregation of instances." Within individual instances, the researcher first looks for examples within a particular subject, in aggregation of instances, the researcher looks across subjects.

1. Topic of Case Study: Perceptions of violence in emergency departments
2. Type of Case Study: Comparative Case Study, also an Instrumental Case Study
3. Methods Used Within Case Study: long, semi-structured interviews with nurses at both hospital sites; self-anchoring scale used with nurses at both hospital sites
4. Research Questions: "How do nurses perceive the threat of violence in the emergency department?"
5. Data Collection: the semi-structured interviews are tiered; the self-anchoring scale is administered prior to the interviews.
6. Data analysis: analysis is begun immediately after a few interviews have been conducted.
   a. The self-anchoring scale is used to inform the interviews and create a picture of the "best" and "worst" hospital emergency department workplaces
   b. Self-anchoring scale data and interview data is analyzed in the following ways
      i. Each individual's data is analyzed by question for themes
      ii. Each individual's data is analyzed as a whole for themes
      iii. Interview data across subjects at one site is analyzed as a whole for themes
      iv. Interview data is analyzed within each individual site for themes
      v. Interview data is analyzed across both sites for themes

Case Study Worksheet

Topic of Case Study:_____

_____

Type of Case Study:_____

_____

Methods Used Within the Case Study:_____

_____

_____

_____

Research Question(s)

1. _____
2. _____
3. _____
4. _____

Data Collection *(spell out for each method of data collection)*

1. _____

_____

_____

_____

_____

2. _____

_____

_____

_____

3. _____

_____

_____

_____

Data Analysis *(include separate analysis for each method of data collection and an integration of all methods)*

1. _____

_____

_____

_____

_____

2. _____

_____

_____

_____

3. _____

_____

_____

_____

4. *(Integration of the other three data points)*_____

_____

_____

_____

_____

Case Study Resources

Baxter, P., & Jack, S. (2008). Qualitative case study methodology: Study design and implementation for novice researchers. *The Qualitative Report, 13* (4), 544-559.

Merriam, S. B. (2009). *Qualitative research: A guide to design and implementation.* San Francisco: John Wiley and Sons.

Miles, M. B., & Huberman, A. M. (1994). *Qualitative data analysis: An expanded source book* (2nd ed.). Thousand Oaks, CA: Sage.

Stake, R. E. (1995). *The Art of Case Study Research.* Thousand Oaks, CA: Sage.

Chapter Three: Phenomenology

The phenomenological study seeks to get at the essence of the phenomenon under study—for example "the lived experience of falling in love for the first time." It seeks to understand what it is like to "fall in love for the first time" from the perspective of the subjects of the study. The goal of this research is to detail for the reader essentially what it is like to be in that experience. These studies are often very moving—allowing the reader a glimpse into the lives of the participants.

There is a long philosophical tradition underpinning phenomenological research, beginning with the works of Edmund Husserl (1857-1938) and Martin Heidegger (1889-1976). Husserl is known for breaking from positivism and the founding of phenomenology. He is responsible for originating the concept of "bracketing" and "epoché" and "phenomenological reduction." His work focused on a "transcendental phenomenology of consciousness." Heidegger was a student of Husserl's and continued his work in phenomenology. Heidegger was concerned not so much with objects in the world, but with examining the essence of being. Out of the roots of phenomenological philosophy came phenomenological psychology and phenomenological sociology.

Phenomenological psychology studies subjective experience and deals with what is termed "Being in the World," where the subject and the world are intertwined—in other words, nothing can be perceived without someone to perceive it. Phenomenological psychology has been strongly influenced by the Duquesne School in Pittsburgh, Pennsylvania and Amedeo Giorgi, who developed the "Descriptive Phenomenological Method" (Giorgi, 2009). Giorgi (http://phenomenologyblog.com/?p=485) stated that at the core of phenomenology is "getting at essences."

Phenomenological sociology is based on the work of Alfred Scheutz. Scheutz brought together Husserl's phenomenological methodology and Max Weber's interpretive sociology (Schutz 1972). Phenomenological sociology examines the social construction of reality by us as beings in the world. It examines everyday life, and the so-called "Life World."

The hallmark of a phenomenological study is that it investigates a phenomenon and focuses on essences. As such, the object of the study needs to rise to the level of a phenomenon. It is often an experience that is at the core of the subject's being. This hallmark is also the key challenge in phenomenology—that you must truly be investigating a phenomenon. You would not want to investigate the "lived experiences of training." "Training" is not a phenomenon. The benefit of phenomenology is the very in-depth engagement that the researcher has with the subjects and the topic under investigation. This makes the approach very appealing to many researchers who want to be very involved with their subjects.

Varieties of Phenomenology

There are two varieties of phenomenology that are widely discussed in the research literature: hermeneutic phenomenology and transcendental phenomenology.

Hermeneutic phenomenology seeks to create authentic descriptions and interpretations of the phenomena. It is focused on the researcher's interpretation of the phenomenon. Transcendental phenomenology (also referred to as empirical phenomenology or psychological phenomenology) has its basis in the structure of shared experiences. It is not focused on the researcher's interpretation of the phenomenon but on the participants' description of the phenomenon.

Phenomenological Data Analysis

In a phenomenological study, the researcher is looking for "meaning units" and "themes" to make sense of the experience of the subject. The analysis begins by the researcher "coding" the data, which allows analyses to follow from that categorization. Giorgi is a great source for phenomenological data analysis, as is Moustakas.

In transcendental phenomenology, the data analysis involves three stages: epoché, transcendental-phenomenological reduction, and imaginative variation. In epoché, the researcher must suspend his or her personal biases to understand the world through the subject. In transcendental-phenomenological reduction, the researcher strives to get at the heart of the object under study. This means going beyond words. Phenomenological reduction is a process to get at how the "noema" (physical world) and "noesis" (experience of the world) are connected. Imaginative variation reveals the hidden by changing the frame of reference, through the use of different perspectives, through looking at different positions and functions. The study moves from a focus on the descriptions of the subjects alone to a general picture of the essence of that experience.

Moustakas (1994) recommends the following steps in data analysis:

1. Horizonalization – highlighting significant statements of the participants' experiences.
2. Clusters of meaning – groupings of the significant statements.
3. Textural description – a description of what the participants experienced based upon the clusters of meaning.
4. Imaginative variation/structural description – A description of the context/setting of the experiences.
5. Essential, invariant structure – derived from the textural and structural descriptions. It is the essence of the phenomenon.

Phenomenology Data Analysis Example

In most phenomenological studies the primary method of data collection will be the long, semi-structured interview.

1. Topic of Phenomenological Study: Experiences of violence in emergency departments
2. Type of Phenomenological Study: Transcendental Phenomenology
3. Method Used Within Phenomenology: long, semi-structured interviews
4. Research Question: "What is the lived experience of threat and violence in the emergency department?"

5. Data Collection: the semi-structured interviews are comprised of guiding interview questions. Each interview lasts at least an hour and focuses on how the subjects experience threat and violence in their work environment.

6. Data analysis: analysis is begun immediately after a few interviews have been conducted and follows Moustakas' (1994) recommended steps: Horizonalization, Clusters of meaning, Textural description, Imaginative variation/structural description, Essential, invariant structure.

Phenomenological Study Worksheet

Topic of Phenomenological Study:_____

_____

Type of Phenomenological Study:_____

_____

Method(s) Used Within the Phenomenological Study:_____

_____

_____

_____

Research Question(s)

1. _____
2. _____

Data Collection *(spell out for each method of data collection)*

1. _____

_____

_____

_____

_____

2. _____

_____

_____

_____

Data Analysis *(include separate analysis for each method of data collection and an integration of all methods)*

1. _____

   _____

   _____

   _____

   _____

2. _____

   _____

   _____

   _____

3. *(Integration of the other data points)*_____

   _____

   _____

   _____

   _____

Phenomenology Resources

Giorgi, A. (2009). *The descriptive phenomenological method in psychology.* Duquesne University Press: Pittsburgh, PA.

Moustakas, C. (1994). *Phenomenological research methods.* Thousand Oaks, CA: Sage.

Miles, M. B, & Huberman, A. M. (1994). *Qualitative data analysis: An expanded handbook* (2nd ed.). Thousand Oaks, CA: Sage.

Phenomenology Blog. (2012, July 16). Amedeo Giorgi: A life in phenomenology. [Web log comment]. Retrieved from http://phenomenologyblog.com/?p=485.

Schutz, A. (1972). *The phenomenology of the social world.* London: Heinemann: Educational Books.

Chapter Four: Generic Qualitative Approaches

Generic qualitative approaches are gaining in popularity and are commonly seen in a variety of diverse disciplines, including healthcare, education, and sociology. This approach is frequently used among practical fields and in practice-oriented research. It does not require the integration of theory. The researcher does not have to abide by the philosophical underpinnings that are required in other qualitative approaches. The researcher does not have to engage in a lengthy qualitative study by can focus solely on the research project at hand and complete the study quickly.

In the literature, this approach is not always referred to as "generic qualitative" but can be found under a variety of names, such as: "interpretive description" (Caelli et al., 2003), "qualitative description" (Caelli et al., 2003), "noncategorical qualitative research" (Thorne, 1997), "fundamental qualitative method" (Sandelowski, 2000), or "generic qualitative method" (Merriam, 1998), among others. In some cases, an article may not specifically name the approach but simply refer to it as a "qualitative study." So when you are conducting your literature review, you will need to be more flexible in your approach to search terms. We have included a number of references to get you started at the end of this chapter.

The hallmark of a generic qualitative study is that it utilizes qualitative methods to answer qualitative research questions, but it does not rely upon the philosophical underpinnings that must underlie the other qualitative approaches. This approach has great flexibility and studies can often be completed in a short amount of time. It is also very appealing to novice researchers—who mistake quickness for ease of completion.

So while the lack of philosophical underpinning can make the researcher's task easier because certain conditions do not have to be met within the research design (like triangulation of data, or investigating a phenomenon), it is also the key challenge in these studies. Without the philosophical underpinnings that underlie other forms of qualitative research, there is little guidance for how to conduct generic qualitative studies. This makes this a particularly difficult approach for novice researchers—who lack experience with all qualitative approaches. It has been suggested by many researchers that structure must be imposed on generic qualitative to make the approach truly viable (Caelli, et al., 2003; Thorne, Kirkham, & MacDonald-Emes, 1997; Sandelowski, 2000). In lieu of a philosophical underpinning to guide the study, researchers who conduct generic qualitative studies should be certain to follow the guidelines that are appropriate for the methods that they are using in the study—whether that is semi-structured interviews, field notes, observations—or any other method to create a structure for the study.

Generic Qualitative Data Analysis

The beginning of any qualitative data analysis is appropriate organization of the data. You will organize the data by method used to collect data. You will need to assign numbers to interviews and organize them by chronology perhaps. I (O'Reilly) organized my own dissertation interviews both by research site and chronologically. Using a letter and a number, I could tell at a glance which site and which subject a transcript was from.

Ritchie and Spencer (1993) recommend a framework approach to data analysis that consists of the following steps:

1. "Familiarization" or being immersed in the data
2. Identifying a thematic framework, looking at key issues, concepts and themes
3. Indexing – creating themes and codes in the data
4. Charting – rearranging the data and creating charts of subject areas
5. Mapping and interpretation – charts may define concepts, typologies may be created

Generic Qualitative Study Data Analysis Example

How generic qualitative study data is analyzed, naturally, depends upon which types of data were collected. This is more important in generic qualitative studies because, of course, it lacks the philosophical underpinnings inherent in the other studies.

1. Topic of Generic Qualitative Study: Lowering the threat of violence in emergency departments
2. Methods Used Within Generic Qualitative Study: long, semi-structured interviews with nurses at both hospital sites; self-anchoring scale used with nurses at both hospital sites; review of hospital incident reports
3. Research Question: "How can the threat of violence in emergency departments be lowered?"
4. Data Collection: incident reports were reviewed; the self-anchoring scale is administered at the start of each interview; semi-structured interviews were conducted.
5. Data analysis: analysis is begun immediately after the incident reports are reviewed.
   a. Incident reports are used to create a chart of when and where violence occurs in the emergency department; also noted is who is most likely to become violent and who is most likely to be a victim.
   b. The self-anchoring scale is used to inform the interviews and create a picture of the "best" and "worst" hospital emergency department workplaces as relates to safety and security.
   c. The interview data is analyzed in the following ways:
      i. When and where do subjects feel most threatened?
      ii. When and where do subjects feel least threatened?
      iii. What would make subjects feel safer?

Generic Qualitative Study Worksheet

Topic of Generic Qualitative Study:_____

_____

Methods Used Within the Generic Qualitative Study:_____

_____

_____

_____

Research Question(s)

1. _____

2. _____

3. _____

4. _____

Data Collection *(spell out for each method of data collection)*

1. _____

_____

_____

_____

_____

2. _____

_____

_____

_____

3. _____

_____

_____

_____

Data Analysis *(include separate analysis for each method of data collection and an integration of all methods)*

1. _____

_____

_____
_____
_____

2. _____
_____
_____
_____

3. _____
_____
_____
_____

4. _(Integration of the other three data points)_____
_____
_____
_____
_____

Generic Qualitative Resources

Caelli K., Ray, L., & Mill, J. (2003). Clear as mud. Towards a greater clarity in generic qualitative research. _International Journal of Qualitative Methods, 2_(2), 1–23.

Merriam, S. B. (1998). Qualitative research and case study applications in education. San Francisco: Jossey-Bass.

Ritchie, J., & Spencer, L. (1993). Qualitative data analysis for applied policy research. In A. Bryman, R. Burgess (Eds.). _Analysing qualitative data_ (pp. 173–194). London: Routledge.

Sandelowski, M. (2000). Whatever happened to qualitative description? _Research in Nursing and Health_, 23, 334–340.

Thorne, S., Kirkham, S. R., & MacDonald-Emes, J. (1997). Interpretive description: A noncategorical qualitative alternative for developing nursing knowledge. _Research in Nursing and Health, 20_, 169–177.

Chapter Five: Ethnography

It has been suggested by some that ethnography is more than just a methodology, more than a specific group of methods, more than a research process, but rather an epistemology—a way of knowing—a philosophy of research (Green, Skukauskaite & Baker, 2011; Agar, 2006; Anderson-Levitt, 2006). Epistemology is the study of knowing—as a branch of philosophy, it concerns itself with "how we know." In research, it has to do with how we acquire our knowledge and what constitutes knowledge. There is a specific epistemology that applies to qualitative in general—that of social constructivism, discussed earlier in this text—the epistemology of ethnography encompasses the epistemology of qualitative but goes further. Agar (2006) holds that ethnography is highly iterative. You do not just move from point A to point B to point C, but move back and forth among points. Ethnography also is in an attempt to understand not only a culture, but also how individuals within that culture live, know, and develop.

The hallmarks of an ethnographic study are that it seeks cultural knowledge and examines a culture, subculture, or micro-culture and that the research must be conducted in the natural setting. It may study a society, a family, a classroom, a social group or a work setting. Ethnographic research will be involved in looking at language, rituals, beliefs, ideals, values, practices and norms to describe that culture, subculture, or micro-culture. A significant portion of the study will take place in the field.

Ethnography has perhaps the longest history and tradition of all of the qualitative approaches. Gerhard Friedrich Mueller, a professor of history and geography, originated this approach during his involvement in the second Kamchatka expedition (1733-1743). During this expedition, he recorded the physical geography of the area and he also commented extensively on the people that were encountered. These two tasks became incorporated into the original conceptualization of ethnography. As ethnography evolved, the focus moved from those things that could be easily observed to intangibles—like values or beliefs.

Ethnographic studies are commonly undertaken in anthropology and sociology. Famous anthropologists include Marcel Mauss (who founded the Institut d'Ethnologie at the University of Paris), Clifford Geertz (who originated the term "thick description"), Claude Levi-Strauss (often referred to as the "Father of Modern Anthropology"), Ruth Benedict (researched culture and personality), Margaret Mead (conceptualized that culture impacts behavior), and Franz Boas (known as the "Father of Modern Cultural Anthropology"). Well-known sociologists of the Chicago School who utilized ethnographic methodology include Nels Anderson ("The Hobo," 1923) and Thomas and Znaniecki ("The Polish Peasant," 1918) (Deegan, 2001). Ethnography appears widely in the social sciences but also in business education, cultural studies, economics, religious studies, history, and communications.

Ethnographic studies seek to be holistic and may examine any of the following:

1. History of the culture
2. Geography where the culture is located
3. Climate where the people in the study live
4. Culture
5. Technology
6. Social structure and social life
7. Language
8. Practices
9. Values
10. Rites and rituals
11. Religion
12. Roles and relationships
13. Norms and expectations
14. Rights and obligations of the members
15. How decisions are made

Interesting Varieties of Ethnography

There are many interesting variations to ethnography—not only within disciplines (like educational ethnography), but also across disciplines, like critical ethnography, focused ethnography, case studies as ethnography, online ethnographies, and autoethnography.

Critical ethnography advocates for marginalized groups. Critical ethnographers advocate for the powerless and against domination and subjugation. Critical ethnography is empowering. Critical ethnography generally puts the research into a political perspective. These studies may be conducted in sociology, social work, and in criminology—or any discipline that has a concern for the powerless or power differentials.

Focused ethnography focuses on a small portion of one's own culture or subculture (Knoblauch, 2005). The key benefit to conducting a focused ethnography is that it will considerably lessen the time needed for the study. While many standard ethnographic studies can take years to complete—a focused ethnography may take months.

It should be noted that some case studies are also ethnographies. If a case study is focusing on a culture, subculture or microculture—it could also be termed as an ethnography. As researchers, we need to keep in mind that the distinctions among the various qualitative approaches are not absolute and there is overlap.

Anthropology is now also studying the internet and online culture (Wittel, 2000). Ethnographies are also being conducted online. Platforms like Second Life provide many opportunities for researchers to study online interactions. Studies can also focus on learning online or use of blogs—to name only a few areas that ethnography may examine.

Autoethnography is autobiographical in nature. In an autoethnographic study, the researcher comments on his or her own experiences, but in light of the wider culture that those experiences are nested within. In this specialized form of ethnography, the researcher must be extra aware of biases—as these will be a portion of the study.

Steps in an Ethnographic Study

1. Gaining permission to enter the research site; obtaining access from gatekeepers.
2. Conducting fieldwork

3. Lengthy observations
4. Document review
5. Interviews are conducted, often multiple interviews with the same subjects
6. Exiting the field

Ethnographers, like all other qualitative researchers, must obtain permission to physically enter the research site; but unlike other qualitative researchers, they must also obtain access from gatekeepers—these are two very different hurdles the researcher must overcome to get into the field. In ethnographic research in education, for example, permission to enter the research site would be given by the state's department of education, the district, and the principal. However, the researcher must also gain access from the gatekeepers, who may be specific teachers or even students (depending upon what the researcher is examining). Permission comes from an official source and is a formal process. Obtaining permission must also be detailed in the IRB paperwork. Gaining access from a gatekeeper is unofficial and much more informal in nature. Gatekeepers are not discussed in the IRB paperwork and, in fact, who the gatekeeper (or gatekeepers) is will not generally be known until the researcher is in the field. There is also risk involved for the researcher in gaining access from the gatekeeper because it is not always obvious who the gatekeeper is at any particular site. This is something that must be learned through careful observation and discussion during fieldwork. If the researcher is not aware of who the gatekeeper is, or chooses the incorrect gatekeeper, the entire research project can bog down very quickly.

Once formal permission to enter the research site is obtained, the fieldwork portion of the study can begin. This is often referred to as "getting into the field." During the initial phases of getting into the field, the researcher will attempt to ascertain who the gatekeeper is at the research site and then obtain access to conduct the research.

Fieldwork is the most difficult portion of the study because it requires lengthy time commitments on the part of both the researcher and the subjects. A researcher may spend years "getting into the field," and the time commitment on a particular subject may be hours, days, or even weeks and months depending upon how extensively that subject is utilized in the research. Some researchers will spend years on this portion of their study alone. It is important that fieldwork is begun without any hypotheses regarding the research setting—without any preconceived notions—so that the researcher is open to whatever the field has to offer. Hypotheses in ethnographic work will arise from the research process itself—not prior to conducting the research. Ethnographers will always conduct observations during fieldwork and, in fact, observations are very important to their work. Unlike other types of qualitative research, which may or may not use observation—observations are a requirement of ethnography.

During fieldwork, informal access will be obtained. A significant portion of getting into the field is conducting qualitative observations and taking field notes. The researcher will conduct extensive qualitative observations. During these observations the researcher will become aware of who the gatekeepers are. The researcher may also develop informants during this phase of the study. These are individuals who are part of the setting and share their stories with the researcher. They may be in key positions within the culture the researcher is studying, or they may simply have a good vantage point. The researcher needs to carefully consider who the informant is prior to utilizing that person as an informant. An informant must be someone who has a vantage point that the researcher needs. The informant must be trustworthy. The researcher should also be aware of the position of the informant within the research setting. An informant of low status or who is looked down upon can negatively impact the researcher's relationship with the rest of the community.

A significant portion of the fieldwork consists of lengthy qualitative observations. Observational data is found in both quantitative and qualitative research—but they are very different. In quantitative observation, the observer is interested in obtaining a count. It may be a count of a certain type of behavior or a count of individuals who are involved in an event—but it is a count nonetheless. Qualitative observation does not merely attempt to obtain a count. It is used to understand the field and how people work, live and relate in that field. It seeks rich description.

In qualitative research, there are three types of observation: pure observation, observer as participant, and participant observation. Each denotes a different type of relationship between the researcher and the observation. In pure observation, the researcher is simply an observer and a recorder of what transpires within the research setting. The researcher is neither a member of the population under study nor is the researcher interacting with the subjects in any way. The easiest way to be a pure observer is to conduct the observations with the researcher wholly isolated from the subjects—for example, behind a two-way mirror. In ethnography, observations are never carried out from a "pure observer" vantage point.

In ethnographic studies, the researcher is most likely to take either an "observer as participant" or "participant observer" stance. If the researcher is conducting observations from an "observer as participant" standpoint, he or she will be involved in the research setting. This may be in the form of standing around and taking notes and asking questions or the researcher may become part of the background of the setting—for example, sitting on a park bench observing subjects playing speed chess. The researcher may also be a "participant observer" and become fully active with the subjects during observation. In anthropology, a participant observer will live with the people he or she is studying; participate in their rituals and ceremonies, eat meals with them, learn their language. The researcher can learn much about the field through participant observation and the observations serve as a check against the reporting of their own subjective experiences done by the subjects. It allows the researcher to gain an understanding from "inside," while still maintaining and "outsider" stance.

Observation in qualitative research may be either overt—where the subjects know that they are being observed, or covert—where the subjects are unaware that they are being observed. Covert observation, unless you are observing in a public place can be viewed as ethically questionable.

Interviews will be conducted with subjects in an ethnographic study—some subjects may be interviewed only briefly—although it is far more common for an individual to be interviewed multiple times. This makes the time commitment necessary from subjects in an ethnographic study higher than that required in other types of qualitative research. Multiple interviews with the same subjects can also be very beneficial as they allow the researcher to ask questions at different stages of the research. (Questions that are important at the outset of a study will not necessarily be the same questions that are important at the middle or toward the end of data collection.) Multiple interviews also allow the researcher to ask about what he or she has seen in the field. It allows questions to be developed as the researcher gains an understanding of the research site. Subjects who serve as "informants" in the research are heavily relied upon during fieldwork and during the interviews to provide significant information about the object of the study.

Ethnography utilizes a wide variety of types of data. This allows the researcher to obtain knowledge of the culture through a variety of means. Multiple types of data also create triangulation and give the study greater credibility. Documents can be reviewed during the fieldwork portion of the study and can range from mission and vision statements for a company to marriage licenses or church records—any documents that are created by people can become potential ethnographic data and the types of documents that will be beneficial to the research vary widely. (Keep in mind, just because a document exists does not mean that it will provide good data for your study.) Documents can be an excellent source of material for ethnographers because the researcher cannot influence documents in the same way that interviews or observations can be influenced by the presence of the researcher. In an ethnographic study of hospital violence, incident reports would be an excellent type of document to include—although they would generally be very difficult to obtain.

Ethnographers also employ methods that are far less frequently used by other qualitative researchers like diaries, photographs, or artifacts. This gives ethnographers a certain degree of freedom to choose the methods that seem most appropriate for the individual studies. Different methods can also be approached in very creative ways during data collection. A pre-existing diary can be used, or the researcher could ask subjects to keep a diary for a period of time during data collection. The researcher could use photographs during data collection as a jumping off point for conversations with subjects—or subjects could be asked to take photographs with cameras of what they feel is important for the researcher to see. Of course, the freedom to choose from all of these methods also presents the difficulty of organizing multiple types of data and analyzing all that data! This is one of the reasons why ethnographic studies take years to complete.

Ethnographic Data Analysis

While all qualitative research creates considerable data, ethnography generally creates the most. This huge volume of data makes the biggest challenge in ethnographic data analysis the organization of all that data. There really is no single "correct" way to analyze data in an ethnographic study, but there is plenty of available literature to assist you in designing your data analysis.

A straightforward approach to ethnographic data analysis consists of first describing what has occurred in the research setting. After description a thematic analysis will be done. The final step is interpretation.

The researcher may look for patterns within the data; some researchers will create typologies—or categorization. Another technique that can be employed is the creation of a sociogram, which is a graphic representation of the social links and relationships within the group that is being studied. It can be much easier to present data visually than in writing, especially when the data has very complex relationships contained within it.

In ethnography, a common approach is to do a thematic analysis, where the interview data is analyzed to see what "themes" are discussed by the subjects. For example, if the research centered on why people volunteer, themes that might arise upon analysis of the interview data could be "personal gratification," "wanting to give back," "wanting to feel needed." The themes are then fitted to patterns that were identified prior to the research being conducted, from the literature. Then, other themes that do not fit previously identified patterns are named.

Roper and Shapira (2000) recommend the following steps for data analysis: coding for descriptive labels, sorting for patterns, identifying outliers, generalizing constructs and theories, memoing with reflective remarks.

The process of analysis begins with coding for descriptive labels. This will take the enormous volume of written material that has been collected and reduce it by grouping it into categories. This makes comparison easier. Codes may be broken down into predetermined domains for ease of sorting. Common domains are: setting, social structure, processes, and events (Roper & Shapira, 2000).

The descriptive labels are then sorted into patterns and themes are developed (Roper & Shapira, 2000). The researcher will identify all data that relates to already classified patterns and perhaps combine related patterns into sub-themes. The researcher may also request feedback from subjects, which increases the credibility of the study. The academic literature is looked to for validation of the themes (Aronson, 1994).

The researcher must identify outliers—cases that do not fit, unusual events or situations (Roper & Shapira, 2000). Unlike quantitative research, which tends to seek to eliminate outliers, for qualitative, outliers may become a key part of the analysis. Since qualitative does not seek to generalize, what one person says may be just as important as what was said by ten people. An outlier may just be an outlier, or it may need to be examined further.

Constructs and theories within the research must be linked back to existing literature in the discipline (Roper & Shapira, 2000). Remember, no research takes place within a vacuum. The literature of the discipline is always important. Prior to the start of the research, the literature will provide a path to follow throughout the research. During the course of the research, the literature will be returned to repeatedly. (Finally, at the end of the research, the write-up will add to the body of literature and extend it.)

Memoing are ideas/feelings/opinions that occur to the researcher that are written down, so that the researcher can follow up later. This is a method of note taking—where the researcher writes down what occurs to him/her throughout the analysis. There are not strict guidelines regarding what is done during memoing. The researcher may jot down questions, make lists of what still needs to be done, discuss personal biases that come to the surface, and write what he or she feels strongly about (Roper & Shapira, 2000).

Challenges of Ethnography

The most significant challenge to an ethnographic study is the time commitment required. There can also be significant barriers to understanding the particular culture or subculture. Many researchers spend months or a year or more in the field before they even being to conduct interviews. It is not easy to understand a culture.

Ethnography, because of the extended and extensive involvement of the researcher also has some serious ethical issues that must be addressed in any study. When a researcher is interested in illegal behaviors and hidden behaviors there are questions as to whether or not the researcher should conduct the research in an overt or covert manner. How involved should a researcher be in the lives of the participants? What if the researcher becomes aware of illegal activities?

Ethnographic researchers also need to be very wary of potential biases on their own part. Being in the field for so long carries the risk that the researcher may "go native" and lose objectivity—and qualitative research is very subjective already.

Ethnographic Study Data Analysis Example

How ethnographic data is analyzed, depends upon which types of data were collected. The researcher must have a clear plan for data collection and data analysis for each type of data. The methods of data collection will be both considered separately and together within the study.

1. Topic of Ethnographic Study: The culture of violent emergency departments

2. Type of Ethnographic Study: Focused Ethnography
3. Methods Used Within Ethnographic Study: short observations and field work to enter the field; long, semi-structured interviews with nurses
4. Research Questions: How do nurses in the emergency department deal with violence and threat in their work environment?
5. Data Collection:
   a. Getting into the field is the first step in the data collection process this will be done through observations not lasting more than one month; extensive field notes will be taken
   b. Semi-structured interviews will be conducted
6. Data analysis: analysis is begun immediately after entering the field and starting the field notes process
   a. Coding for descriptive labels
   b. Sorting for patterns
   c. Identifying outliers
   d. Generalizing constructs and theories
   e. Memoing with reflective remarks.

Ethnographic Study Worksheet

Topic of Ethnographic Study:_____

_____

Type of Ethnographic Study:_____

_____

Methods Used Within the Ethnographic Study:_____

_____

_____

_____

Research Question(s)

1. _____
2. _____
3. _____
4. _____

Data Collection *(spell out for each method of data collection)*

1. _____

_____

_____

_____

_____

2. _____

_____

_____

_____

3. _____

_____

_____

_____

Data Analysis *(include separate analysis for each method of data collection and an integration of all methods)*

1. _____

_____

_____

_____

_____

2. _____

_____

_____

_____

3. _____

_____

_____

_____

4. *(Integration of the other three data points)*_____

_____

_____

_____

_____

Ethnography Resources

Agar, M. (2006). An ethnography by any other name.... *Forum Qualitative Sozialforschung/Forum: Qualitative Social Research*, 7(4), Art. 36. Retrieved from http://nbn-resolving.de/urn:nbn:de:0114-fqs0604367.

Anderson, N. (1923). *The hobo: The sociology of the homeless man.* Chicago: University of Chicago Press.

Anderson-Levitt, K. (2006). Ethnography. In J. L. Green, G. Camilli, & P. B. Elmore (eds.) *Handbook of complementary methods in education research* (pp. 279–96). Mahwah, NJ: Lawrence Erlbaum.

Aronson, J. (1994). A pragmatic view of thematic analysis. *The Qualitative Report*, 2, (1), 1-3.

Deegan, M. J. (2001). The Chicago school of ethnography. In P. Atkinson, A. Coffey, S. Delamont, J. Lofland, & L. Lofland (eds.) *Handbook of ethnography* (pp. 11-25). Thousand Oaks, CA: Sage.

Green, J. L., Skukauskaite, A., & Baker, W. D. (2011). Ethnography as Epistemology. Research Methods and Methodologies in Education.

Knoblauch, H. (2005). Focused Ethnography. *Forum Qualitative Sozialforschung / Forum: Qualitative Social Research*, 6(3), Art. 44. Retrieved from http://www.qualitative-research.net/index.php/fqs/article/view/20/43

Roper, J. M., & Shapira, J. (2000). *Ethnography in nursing research.* Thousand Oaks, CA: Sage. Thomas, W. I., & Znaniecki, F. (1918). *The Polish peasant in Europe and America.* Chicago: University of Chicago Press.

Wittel, A. (2000). Ethnography on the move: From field to net to internet. *Forum Qualitative Sozialforschung / Forum: Qualitative Social Research*, 1(1), Art. 21. Retrieved from http://www.qualitative-research.net/index.php/fqs/article/view/1131/2517

Chapter Six: Grounded Theory

The hallmark of a grounded theory study is that the researcher creates a theory from the "ground up." In grounded theory, the theory is data driven—data is collected first, and then from the data, theory is created. This is in contrast to theories created prior to gathering data—simply by hypothesizing about the world—which is how the majority of theories are created.

Ideally, a grounded theory approach is is chosen when current theories are not appropriately explaining how something in the world works. This presents a challenge for students because it not only requires that the researcher first be familiar with all possible theories in his or her own discipline but also with theories in other disciplines—at least in the Strassian form of grounded theory. Because of the knowledge of other theories that is required, seasoned researchers and theoreticians who have been active in the academic side of the discipline for many years create most new theories.

The Beginnings of Grounded Theory

Grounded theory was developed by Barney Glaser and Anselm Strauss in their sociological study of dying patients. Their study resulted first in the publication of *Awareness of Dying* in 1965 and then in the publication of *The Discovery of Grounded Theory* in 1967. In *Awareness of Dying*, Glaser and Strauss created a theory about the management of information surrounding a patient's terminal illness. It examined what patients know about their illness and what is told to them about their illness. (Keep in mind that dying had not been studied much as of 1965; Kubler Ross' book, *On Death and Dying*, was still four years away.) Glaser and Strauss examined a subject that had little to no literature (this lack of literature—or having read the literature—is key to Glaserian Grounded Theory) and from the data that they obtained through talking to a variety of stakeholders (patients, family members of patients, medical personnel), they created a new theory where none existed before. Although Glaser and Strauss worked together early on after key differences in their views of what grounded theory should be, they have each developed their own school of grounded theory: Glaserian grounded theory and Straussian grounded theory.

Glaserian Grounded Theory

It should be noted that Glaserian grounded theory is seen as being closer to the original conceptualization of grounded theory. In Glaserian grounded theory, the researcher must begin without any preconceived notions about what will be discovered during the research process. The literature of the discipline should not be reviewed prior to the write-up of the data. The researcher must be passive and use neutral questions—again, no preconceived notions in the questions asked.

Glasser considers that "all is data." This approach to grounded theory should not just be considered to be a qualitative approach that is bound to using only qualitative methods. It is free to utilize quantitative methods as well. This allows considerable flexibility regarding what is collected as data. Data analysis begins immediately in Glaserian grounded theory—this is referred to as the "constant comparative method" and allows the researcher to continually return to the subjects and the data for confirmation of the theory that is emerging from the data.

In Glaserian grounded theory, social processes will be identified—whereas this will not always be the case in Straussian grounded theory. In Glaserian grounded theory, theory creation is purely inductive in nature—meaning theory arises out of particular observations (data).

The great danger in Glaserian grounded theory is that unskilled researchers can very easily wind up with theories that do not move the discipline forward—either because their new theories are not well-constructed or because the "new" theory really isn't so new after all. Without grounding in the literature, novices may very well create something that already exists—and because they are new to the discipline, they will be unaware that they have, in effect, "reinvented the wheel." Another danger lies in the fact that the Glaserian approach provides very little guidance or structure regarding data analysis—again, this can leave a novice researcher stumbling in the dark.

Straussian Grounded Theory

While Glaserian grounded theory has a very open and unstructured approach to theory creation, Straussian grounded theory provides more structure to the novice researcher and theoretician. In Straussian grounded theory, the researcher should have a general idea of where to start with the research. This is through a thorough reading of the pre-existing literature and a significant background in both the theories within the discipline and the theories outside of the discipline that could apply to the object under study. In Strassian grounded theory, the researcher is active and will utilize structured questions. The resultant theory will be interpreted by the researcher. Basic social process need not be identified.

Data analysis consists primarily of three types of coding: open, axial, and selective. In Strassian grounded theory, just as in Glaserian grounded theory, the researcher conducts a constant-comparative analysis, where he or she will move back and forth from the data collection to the coding to theory development. The first step is to open code all of the data as it is collected. This allows the researcher to literally code everything. In axial coding, the researcher will relate the codes that were arrived at during the open coding process to each other. Finally, in selective coding, the researcher will choose one code to be the core code and relate everything else within the data to that core code.

An important distinction from Glaserian grounded theory is that Strassian grounded theory stresses that deduction, validation, and verification are important. Strassian grounded theory continues to evolve and change—whereas Glasser asserts that Glaserian grounded theory has not changed.

Grounded Theory Data Analysis

Grounded theory data analysis. A variety of methods of data collection can be used in grounded theory—from interviewing to reviewing historical documents. The data analysis will depend upon what types of data are being reviewed. In general, the process of grounded theory flows from identifying codes, to identifying concepts, then to categories, and—

finally—creating a theory. The works of Glaser, Strauss, and Corbin should be reviewed by anyone considering a grounded theory study.

Data is analyzed using the constant comparative method. Then, a core category is identified. This core category may be a model or theory or process and serve to create a rich theory. More interviews (up to 50 or 60) are conducted within a grounded theory study than within other qualitative studies.

The final theory should be evaluated by its fit, relevance, workability, and modifiability (Glaser & Strauss, 1967). The concepts developed in the theory should "fit" with whatever they represent, and this should be confirmed by the subjects. The study should be "relevant" to the participants and not purely academic in nature—again, confirmed by the subjects. The theory must "work" as an explanation of the problem. Finally, the theory must be modifiable and can be altered when new data becomes available.

Grounded Theory Study Data Analysis Example

How ground theory study data is analyzed, naturally, depends upon which types of data were collected and on whether you choose to follow the Glasserian or Straussian version of grounded theory.

1. Topic of Grounded Theory Study: Acceptable and Unacceptable Violence
2. Type of Grounded Theory Study: Straussian grounded theory
3. Methods Used Within Grounded Theory Study: review of hospital incident reports; self anchoring scale administered to subjects prior to interviews; long, semi-structured interviews with nurses.
4. Research Questions: "What constitutes acceptable and unacceptable violence in the emergency department?"
5. Data Collection: review of hospital incident reports; administering self-anchoring scales; administering semi-structured interviews to 50 nurses.
6. Data analysis: analysis is begun immediately after the incident reports have been obtained
   a. The incident reports are used to create an official picture of the violence within the emergency department
   b. The self-anchoring scales creates a picture of the most and least violent hospital emergency departments possible
   c. The semi-structured interviews allow subjects to speak about what is "acceptable" and "unacceptable" violence.
      i. Open coding of all data—this is done during the data collection process, everything is coded
      ii. Axial coding—codes are related to each other
      iii. Selective coding—finally one core code is derived

Grounded Theory Study Worksheet

Topic of Grounded Theory Study:_____

_____

Type of Grounded Theory Study:_____

_____

Methods Used Within the Grounded Theory Study:_____

_____

_____

_____

Research Question(s)

1. _____

2. _____

3. _____

4. _____

Data Collection *(spell out for each method of data collection)*

1. _____

_____

_____

_____

_____

2. _____

_____

_____

_____

3. _____

_____

_____

_____

Data Analysis *(include separate analysis for each method of data collection and an integration of all methods)*

1. _____

_____

_____

_____

_____

2. _____

_____

_____

_____

3. *(Integration of the other data points)*_____

_____

_____

_____

_____

Grounded Theory Resources

Glaser, B., & Strauss, A. (1965). *Awareness of dying.* Chicago, IL: Aldine Publishing.

Glaser, B., & Strauss, A. (1967). The discovery of grounded theory: Strategies for Qualitative Research. Chicago: Aldine.

Kuebler-Ross, E. (1969). *On death and dying.* London: Routledge.

Morse, J. M., Stern, P. N., Corbin, J. M., Bowers, B., & Clarke, A. E. (2009). *Developing grounded theory: The second generation.* Walnut Creek, CA: University of Arizona Press.

Chapter Seven: Narrative

Narrative analysis can stand alone as a qualitative approach—or it can be used as a technique to analyze verbal data within other qualitative approaches. It is not uncommon to perform a narrative analysis in a phenomenological or a grounded theory study. Narrative analysis arose out of a lack of human stories in the literature of the social sciences—and the need for these stories to communicate what it is like to be a human being. Stories are what human experience is all about (McCormack, 2000). While quantitative approaches may allow for generalizability to a wider population—they do not tell us much about the stories of the subjects. Quantitative methods do not situate its variables within the broader story of humanity—narrative analysis does.

Narrative analysis employs the descriptions of experiences to explain the object of the research study and allows subjects to tell their own stories. It can focus either on an individual or on a group. In all cases, the researcher will extract meaning from the text of the narratives. The hallmark of narrative is, of course, the story. Whatever is being studied must lend itself to a story. Approaches like life history and biography are ideal for the narrative approach. The obvious benefit to this approach is its flexibility—if it can tell a story, it can be approached narratively. However, it can be difficult to know when you are done collecting data since the boundaries of narrative can become very blurry. It can also be more challenging to work with visual data (photographs or artwork) as opposed to verbal data.

Data Collection in Narrative Analysis

Data collection in narrative centers on interviews and other methods that allow for stories to be told, for example, videos, photographs, and participant observation (Riessman, 2008). Common methods used in this approach include field notes, journals, letters, photos, family stories, life histories, oral histories, biographies and autobiographies. This approach can also be used with online artifacts like blogs, e-mails, and texts.

Narrative Data Analysis

Because narrative research is all about the story that an individual tells, the central concern of narrative data analysis is organizing and making sense of that story. Stories may be analyzed thematically, structurally, dialogically, linguistically, visually, biographically, or psychologically.

- A thematic analysis categorizes the data by "themes" or "codes." Thematic analyses are not exclusive to narrative research, but are also commonly used in case study and grounded theory. (Riessman, 2008)
- In a structural analysis, you will examine how the subject constructs the story and focus on the parts of the story. Structural analysis examines the structure of the data—the ways that the stories are told (Riessman, 2008).

- Dialogic analysis examines the way in which people talk to each other (Riessman, 2008). This has been used in a variety of diverse settings, including psychiatry (Martinez, Tomicic, & Medina, 2012) and organizational learning (Oswick, Anthony, Keenoy, Mangham, & Grant, 2000).

- A linguistic analysis puts the analytical emphasis not only on the words being used, but also how they are used and words that are not used.

- A biographical analysis attempts to tell the story of a person's life—or a part of that life.

- Visual analysis is a growing form of analysis that can encompass diverse visual forms such as art, photographs, videos, and computer media (Riessman, 2008).

- Psychological analysis examines motives and meaning behind the story and behind the individual's actions.

McCormack (2000) admits that researchers who utilize a narrative approach have a daunting task in front of them when it comes to data analysis. The point of the data analysis is to turn the transcript data into a meaningful story—which can be very difficult considering the mountains of data that the study might create. McCormack (2000) recommends viewing the transcripts through the multiple lenses of active listening, narrative processes, language, context, and moments. Finally, she suggests using all that to write interpretive stories.

Active listening is about being acquainted with the data and being immersed in the transcripts. The researcher should listen to the tapes repeatedly and then try to make sense out of what the subjects have said. The researcher should also reflect upon his or her own assumptions and biases. The researcher considers who the subject is and how the subject is situated in the world. (McCormack, 2000).

The lens of narrative processes has the researcher examining the verbal tools used by the subject to express his or her story. McCormack (2000) lists stories, description, argumentation, augmentation, and theorizing as potential narrative processes. The subject may simply be telling a story—or she may be describing—or he may be arguing for a particular point of view—or she may be supplementing other information—or he may be trying to explain and make sense out of what has happened.

The lens of language has the researcher examine the use of language. The researcher will pay attention to what the subjects say, how they say it, and what the subjects do not say (McCormack, 2000). Sometimes it is more important what is left out of the story—what is not in the transcripts.

The lens of context will examine both culture and the situation the subject is situated in (McCormack, 2000). The researcher must take into account gender and race, social status, ethnic group, sexual orientation. We must be sensitive to in groups and out groups, power differentials, and how individuals within the culture or situation under study may present themselves.

The lens of moments may consist of memories, turning points, and surprises (McCormack, 2000). These can be key to any subject's story and can also provide great information for the researcher to highlight. For any particular subject, it can be helpful to try to highlight several moments for inclusion in the final write-up. You may want to consider for each of your subjects: "What is the turning point in their story?"

The final step of the narrative analysis is to write an interpretive story—making sense of the whole of the data (McCormack, 2000). The interpretive story goes beyond mere regurgitation of the interviews and bridges the gap between the subjects' stories and the academic literature.

Narrative Study Data Analysis Example

1. Topic of Narrative Study: Nurses' stories of violence in the emergency department
2. Methods Used Within the Narrative Study: long, semi-structured interviews with nurses
3. Research Questions: "How do nurses tell the story of violence in the emergency department?"
4. Data Collection: semi-structured interviews
5. Data analysis: thematic analysis is conducted
   a. Each individual's data is analyzed by question for themes
   b. Each individual's data is analyzed as a whole for themes
   c. Interview data across subjects is analyzed as a whole for themes

Qualitative software

There are a variety of different qualitative software packages on the market, including:
- ATLAS ti (http://www.atlasti.com/qualitative-software.html),
- MAXQDA (http://www.maxqda.com/), and
- NVivo (http://www.qsrinternational.com/)

to name a few. Unlike quantitative software, qualitative software is not designed to analyze your qualitative data, but rather to help organize your data to make the analysis and write-up easier. Since much of qualitative data is written, and qualitative approaches like narrative can generate a considerable amount of data, organization of that data is perhaps the most important thing that you can do during your study to make analysis and write-up easier. Qualitative software is especially useful for organizing themes and codes. You can also use it to categorize quotes from your subjects.

The use of qualitative software is very much a personal decision. Many qualitative researchers prefer to analyze their data the old fashion way—by hand, through the use of notecards, or a bulletin board. Qualitative software usually has a cost attached to it, whereas the cost of notecards is very minimal. Qualitative software may also keep you at a distance from your data—whereas the use of notecards can foster more interaction with your data. The choice is yours.

Narrative Study Worksheet

Topic of Narrative Study:_____

_____

Type of Narrative Study:_____

_____

Methods Used Within the Narrative Study:_____

_____

_____

_____

Research Question(s)

1. _____

2. _____

3. _____

4. _____

Data Collection *(spell out for each method of data collection)*

1. _____

_____

_____

_____

_____

2. _____

_____

_____

_____

3. _____

_____

_____

_____

Data Analysis *(include separate analysis for each method of data collection and an integration of all methods)*

1. _____

_____

_____

_____

2. _____

_____

_____

_____

3. _____
   _____
   _____
   _____

4. *(Integration of the other three data points)*_____
   _____
   _____
   _____
   _____

Narrative Resources

Atkinson, A. and Delamont, S. (Eds.) (2006). *Narrative methods.* London: Sage.

Bal, M. (1997). *Narratology: Introduction to the theory of narrative.* Toronto: University of Toronto Press.

Dibley, L. (2011). Analysing narrative data using McCormack's lenses. *Nurse Researcher, 18*(3), 13–19.

Martinez, C., Tomicic, A., & Medina, L. (2012). Dialogic discourse analysis of psychotherapeutic dialogue: microanalysis of relevant psychotherapy episodes. *International Journal for Dialogical Science, 6*(1), 99-121.

McCormack, C. (2000). From interview transcript to interpretive story: Part 1 – Viewing the transcript through multiple lenses. *Field Methods, 12*(4), 282–297.

Oswick, C., Anthony, P., Keenoy, T., Mangham, I. L., & Grant, D. (2000). A dialogic analysis of organizational learning." *Journal of Management Studies,37*, 887–902.

Riessman, C. K. (2008). *Narrative methods for the human sciences.* Thousand Oaks, CA: Sage Publications.

Chapter Eight: Critical and Action Research

You will notice as you read this chapter that within the categories of critical research and action research there is considerable overlap and similarities. Critical research and action research both arose to address a perceived serious flaw in traditional research approaches—that traditional research remains removed from the subjects and from practical application. While traditional research has as its goal to study and understand a problem, the goal of critical research and action research is to go beyond merely understanding a problem and make a positive change in the lives of the subjects. Perhaps the key benefit of action research is that it allows the researcher to be a change agent—rather than just observing or studying a particular problem.

Critical Research

Critical research is intimately linked to critical theory and other critical approaches. It is named "critical" because it is just that—critical of traditional research approaches. As was mentioned early in this text, positivism (the paradigm behind quantitative research) was the dominant paradigm in research since the enlightenment. During the 1960s and 1970s, social constructivism (the paradigm behind qualitative) arose as an alternative to positivism. Critical theory arose as an alternative to both positivism and social constructivism. And while positivism and social constructivism are associated with a particular methodology (quantitative and qualitative respectively), critical theory is not wedded to either methodology, but rather has different goals than either of these paradigms. Critical research has as its goal the empowerment of its subjects and the examination of power differentials. Critical research is often carried out through participatory action research.

Action Research

Action research is becoming increasingly population in practice-oriented fields like healthcare, education, and organizational development. The focus of action research is practice and not scholarship. It takes a problem in a work environment or social setting and develops and implements a plan of action to address that problem. At its most basic, it is a problem solving effort (Meyer, 2000).

Action researchers strive to be more involved in their research and in the world than traditional researchers. They view the research process as a collaborative process, where the subjects drive the research. The researcher must be engaged with the subjects and create a working dialogue (Reason, & Bradbury, 2006).

Various Types of Action Research

Action research continues to grow and change. As such, there is no definitive list of types of action research. You need to be aware that different authors may even use different names to refer to essentially the same type of action research, but some of the more common types are as follows:

- Traditional Action Research - Kurt Lewin originated the term action research in his 1946 study on race relations. In his article, Lewin hailed his study as a change experiment. He saw great promise for what he viewed as the cooperation between social scientists and practitioners. He viewed action research as this bridge between scholars and practitioners. Lewin worked within organizations to effect change.

- Participatory Action Research – In participatory action research, the researcher takes an active part in changing something. This is common in healthcare research.

- Radical Action Research - Comes from Marxism. Focuses on power. There is also Feminist Action Research.

- Educational Action Research (Action Learning) - Came from the writings of John Dewey who believed that educators should become involved in community problem-solving. The thrust of action learning is of individuals coming together to learn from each other's experiences.

Ethical Challenges in Critical Research and Action Research

In general, qualitative research, because of how closely it deals with subjects has more potential ethical challenges than quantitative research. Of the qualitative approaches—action research and critical research have the greatest potential for ethical challenges, including: bias, dual relationships, and subjectivity.

Because action researchers are often researching their own workplaces, there is a great potential for bias. In other types of research, researchers are cautioned *not* to conduct research in their own workplace because of the potential for bias, but in action research, the researcher purposefully conducts research in his or her own workplace. Action researchers believe that individuals in the problem situation are the ones who are best able to create a solution to that problem, thus objectivity is not the goal.

Dual relationships are almost impossible to avoid in critical research and action research. Most individuals who undertake critical research or action research are either a part of the setting where the research is being conducted or they are very close to it. Again, the critical research-action research paradigm, rather than shy away from dual relationships embraces them.

Because of the intimate involvement of the researcher with the research process, with the subjects in the research, and with the object of the research, critical researchers and action researchers do not strive for objectivity. In fact, objectivity stands in opposition to the whole philosophy behind critical research and action research.

Conducting Critical Research and Action Research

Conducting critical research and action research requires a completely different mindset than all other research. It simply is not like other research—not even other qualitative research. Both critical research and action research are emergent processes (Reason & Bradbury, 2006). While the researcher will begin with a plan, that plan must be a living plan created in collaboration with the subjects—who might more appropriately be referred to as "co-researchers." The research will change as needed during the research process as the researchers gain knowledge about the problem that is being examined.

Action research embraces all qualitative methods and will also utilize quantitative methods if appropriate. Rather than remain rooted within either the qualitative or quantitative paradigm, action research will use whatever methods are appropriate and necessary to solve the problem. What is necessary is that action research be conducted in a natural setting and not in the contrived laboratory setting.

Conducting an action research study is not a linear process like most quantitative and qualitative studies. It is sometimes conceived as a circular process or a spiral process (Kemmis & McTaggart, 2000; O'Leary, 2004; Susman, 1983) conducting proposes the following steps: diagnosing, action planning, taking action, evaluating, specific learning.

1. Diagnosing consists of determining what problem needs to be addressed.
2. In action planning, an intervention will be designed.
3. During taking action, the intervention will be carried out.
4. In evaluating, the outcomes of intervention will be measured.
5. Finally, in specific learning, the research will make note of what has been learned during the entire process.
6. The process begins again.

Because of the circular or spiral nature of action research, it can be difficult to know when to end the research. At some point, the researcher must decide that the research has come to an end and move from the research endeavor into continuous process improvement.

Action Research Study Data Analysis Example

Once more we will turn to our study and this time approach it as an action research study. If this study were conducted as an action research study, the researcher would most likely work as a nurse within the hospital emergency department that is the site for the study.

1. Diagnosis of the problem: violence within the emergency department.
2. Topic of Action Research Study: Addressing the Problem of Violence in Hospital Emergency Departments
3. Type of Action Research Study: Participatory Action Research
4. Action Planning: an intervention will be designed
5. Methods Used Within Action Research Study: long, semi-structured interviews with nurses
6. Data Collection: semi-structured interviews with nurses to determine what situations pose the most risk and how they can be made to feel safer
7. Taking Action: the intervention will be carried out.
8. Evaluating the outcomes: intervention will be measured.
   a. Do the nurses feel safer? Why or why not?
9. Specific Learning: the research will make note of what has been learned during the entire process.
10. The process will repeat to continue to make the work environment safer.

Action Research Study Worksheet

Diagnosis of the Problem:_____

_____

Topic of Action Research Study:_____

_____

Type of Action Research Study:_____

_____

Action Planning:_____

_____

_____

_____

Methods Used Within the Action Research Study

1. _____

2. _____

3. _____

Research Question(s)

1. _____

2. _____

3. _____

4. _____

Data Collection *(spell out for each method of data collection)*

1. _____

   _____

   _____

   _____

   _____

2. _____

   _____

3. _____
_____
_____
_____
_____

Taking Action *(carrying out the intervention)*:_____
_____
_____
_____
_____

Evaluating the Outcomes *(measure the intervention)*

1. _____
_____
_____
_____
_____

2. _____
_____
_____
_____

3. _____
_____
_____
_____

Specific Learning:_____
_____
_____
_____
_____

Repeat the Process:_____

_____

_____

_____

_____

Critical and Action Research Resources

Kemmis, S., & McTaggart, R. (2000). Participatory action research: Communicative action and the public sphere. In N. K. Denzin & Y. S. Lincoln, *Handbook of qualitative research.* Thousand Oaks, CA: Sage Publications.

Lewin, K. (1946). Action Research and Minority Problems. *Journal of Social Issues. 2*,34–46.

Meyer, J. (2000). Using qualitative methods in health related action research. *British Medical Journal, 320*, 178–181.

O'Leary, Z. (2004). The essential guide to doing research. London: Sage.

Reason, P., & Bradbury, H. (2008). The SAGE Handbook of Action Research: Participative Inquiry and Practice (2nd edition). London: Sage.

Susman, G. (1983). Action Research: A Sociotechnical Systems Perspective. In G. Morgan (Ed.) Beyond Method: Strategies for Social Research (pp. 95–113). Newbury Park, CA: Sage Publications.

PART THREE –
METHODS AND CHALLENGES

The final part to this book covers a variety of methods utilized in qualitative research—although it is not meant to be exhaustive, of course. Qualitative offers great flexibility in the methods it will allow. This final part of the text also discusses the overall challenges of creating and conducting a qualitative study, focusing on ethical issues, and also on feasibility.

Sampling in Qualitative Research

All research, whether it is quantitative or qualitative, is interested in a particular population. Because it is generally impossible to access the entire population, researchers look at a "sample" of that population—which is a subset of individuals from the population. In quantitative, the sample is used to generalize to the larger population. To increase the likelihood of generalizability, some studies use probability sampling and a random sample. (It should be noted that this is not always possible, especially in the social sciences, so many studies will use non-probability, convenience sampling.) In qualitative, the point is never to generalize to a larger population, so sampling is approached differently. Qualitative studies almost always utilize non-probability, convenience sampling. In non-probability, convenience sampling, subjects are chosen because they have certain qualities—perhaps they are police officers, or homeless individuals. They are also chosen because they are available—they have volunteered, they live near the researcher, they are undergraduate psychology students.

Chapter Nine: Qualitative Methods

A "method" is a way of gathering data for research. A method may be qualitative or quantitative. This chapter discusses interviews, observations, field notes, documents and artifacts. Interviews, observations and field notes are common qualitative methods used to collect data. Documents and artifacts could be considered to be "types of qualitative methods".

Data that is collected may be analyzed in a variety of ways; the choice of how the data in your study is analyzed is up to you. You will spend considerable time reading in the methodological literature about different ways to analyze data before you design your own research. Your discipline will impact how you analyze your data; sociology may recommend different ways of analyzing data, as opposed to education or criminal justice. Your analysis will also be guided by your qualitative approach—data in a phenomenological study may be analyzed very differently than in a case study because the two approaches have different goals.

Interviews

The most common way of collecting data in qualitative research is through the use of the long interview. The heart and soul of much qualitative research lies in the interview because this is the way in which our subjects speak to us—both literally and figuratively. We come to understand their world, their experience, and their perceptions though our interaction with them in the interview process. Also, keep in mind that you should strive to tape-record all of your interviews. Although this may make some subjects uncomfortable, this is necessary for most types of analysis.

Interview Skills

If you are going to use interviews as a method of data collection in your qualitative research, you must seek out training in interviewing. Interviewing skills are soft skills. Always remember it is a human interaction and you need to be present with your subject as a human being. Even if you have been working in a profession that requires you to conduct other sorts of interviews (clinical interviewing for example, or journalistic interviewing, or even police interviewing), the research interview has different goals than other types of interviews. So while the goal of a therapeutic interview is to learn about the concern of the client that brings him or her to counseling and the goal of an investigative interview is to discover what happened during a crime, the goal of a research interview is to obtain data from the subject. You will need to hone your ability to establish rapport with your subjects, to be empathetic, to ask questions and to listen to responses.

To obtain good qualitative data, especially during long semi-structured or unstructured interviews, establishing a good rapport with your subjects is very important. Creating positive rapport with your subjects begins before the interview with how you present your recruitment materials to subjects. Subjects must feel valued and respected as you approach them to be in the study, whether that contact is via e-mail, phone call or in person. At all stages of the interview process, the researcher should be mindful of the Belmont Report's requirement of "respect for persons." Respect for persons requires that all subjects are treated as autonomous individuals, able to make their own decisions. Subjects must also be treated with courtesy and must be fully informed of the risks and benefits of participating in the research study.

Rapport can be fostered or damaged by who you are personally, how you present yourself—down to what you wear to the interview. If female rape survivors are to be interviewed, having a male interviewer them might be a bad idea. If you are interviewing medical doctors, you would want to wear professional clothing; on the other hand, if you are interviewing homeless individuals, it might be better to dress casually.

Rapport can be built through the structure of the interview itself. Each interview should start off with non-threatening, rapport-building questions; the creation of the interview will be discussed shortly. At the opening of the interview, you must appropriately set the stage for what is to come. You need to explain the purpose of the interview, including confidentiality and consent. You should set an expectation regarding the length of the interview. It is also important to allow the subject to ask you questions before you begin the interview. Rapport can be enhanced by a comfortable and safe interview space. Chairs should be comfortable; the space should be well lit and free from distractions. For example, if you are interviewing subjects about their employer, it could be uncomfortable for them to speak with you at their workplace.

Rapport must be maintained throughout the interview so that subject responses are as open and honest as possible. As the interview progresses, you should be non-judgmental and empathetic toward your subjects. Depending upon the subject matter of the research, you may hear many surprising, unusual, even horrible things in the context of an interview. Any reaction you show should be geared toward trying to understand the experiences of the subject without judgment.

As you go through the individual interview, you need to ask questions clearly and not too quickly. Even if your subjects have normal hearing, you must still speak more slowly than you would during normal conversation. The pacing of your questions must be such that your subjects will have time to think about their responses and then respond. Do not be afraid of silences of 10-20 seconds. You must also be engaged in active listening during the interview. Don't focus on asking the next question, focus on hearing the current response. You may need to ask follow-up questions or use prompts to obtain richer information. A subject may say something unexpected and you need to be able to explore the unexpected— it is these gems that are the real heart of qualitative interviewing.

Types of interviews

There are two broad categories of qualitative interviews: the semi-structured interview and the unstructured interview. The unstructured interview, as the name implies, has no predetermined structure. It does not consist of a number of questions that you will ask the subjects, but relies upon you allowing the subject to respond to perhaps one or two very focused questions. It is most often used when compiling life histories in sociology. The unstructured interview can be very difficult for the new researcher to use because of that lack of structure. While the lack of structure can allow the subject to speak freely of his or her own experience, some subjects are less verbose than others and the unstructured interview may fall flat. The unstructured interview is most often used when compiling life histories in sociology.

Most interviews that are conducted in qualitative studies are semi-structured in nature. The semi-structured interview generally consists of 10-15 questions that are meant to guide the interview. The interview questions allow the interview to be guided without being too directive. The semi-structured interview, while still requiring quite a bit of skill to conduct, is far less challenging than the unstructured interview.

Whether you are conducting unstructured or semi-structured interviews, multiple interviews can be done with the same subjects. This may be done to increase credibility, as a method of member-checking. It can also be done so that you can return to earlier subjects later on in the research process when you have different questions for them. One of the things to be aware of is the time-commitment that this takes both on the part of the researcher and on the part of the subjects. If you want to interview the same individuals more than once, be aware that this may discourage some subjects from participating.

You may also want to consider using a tiered approach to interviewing. A tiered interview is conducted in stages to help you continue to develop the interview questions as the research progresses. You conduct your interview with several subjects and then make changes to the interview schedule based upon how the questions are eliciting information or if you have found different areas to explore based upon what the initial subjects have mentioned.

You may also want to consider conducting focus groups as a method of data collection. A focus group interview is an interview that is conducted with a group of subjects simultaneously. It should not be considered to be multiple interviews conducted at once, but it is a very different animal and requires its own special skill set. If you are going to attempt to conduct focus groups, you will, as with any data collection technique, want to educate yourself as much as possible about this technique.

Conducting a focus group is very different than conducting individual interviews. You will need to consider group dynamics in your interview. Some individuals may attempt to dominate the conversation, while others may try to remain silent. Rather than you, as interviewer, developing a relationship with each individual, you must develop a relationship with the group as a whole. It is often recommended that the researcher hire a person skilled in conducting focus groups to guide the sessions, while the researcher takes notes during the interview process. Another problem that presents itself during the analysis of focus group data is that the data is not analyzed individually—but must be analyzed for the group. In certain cases, focus groups may be inappropriate, such as when sensitive topics like dealing with violence or sexuality are being discussed.

Forum for Conducting the Interview

There are a variety of ways that you can conduct your interview, including: face-to-face, telephone, Voice over Internet Protocol (VoIP), virtual reality, and online text. Each forum, of course, has pros and cons.

Face-to-face. There are many benefits to the face-to-face interview. You will be able to observe the subjects reaction to your questions and make note of nonverbal cues. This can provide a lot more information that the verbal data from the interview alone. It may also be easier to develop rapport in person. Focus groups should be conducted in a face-to-face format. However, face-to-face interviews also take considerable skill. It can be difficult to interview and take notes—as your note taking will generally be fairly obvious to the subjects.

Telephone. Telephone interviews will not allow you the same opportunity to build rapport with your subjects as face-to-face interviews do. You will lose the ability to see their body language and facial expressions. You also will not be able to guarantee that your subject will be distraction-free or that no one will overhear their end of the conversation, which in the case of some sensitive topics (like domestic violence) could put your subject at risk. You also may not be able to provide your subject easy access to services if needed. Telephone interviews do, however, allow you to overcome geographical challenges. So, if you must interview subjects from a great distance and you cannot drive or fly to the interview sites, this can be a viable option. During a telephone interview, you can take notes without the subjects noticing more easily, you can also follow your interview guide more easily.

Voice Over Internet Protocol (VoIP). VoIP is a means of delivering voice and media over the Internet, for example Skype and Google Talk. It is becoming far more common to conduct interviews in this manner as more and more individuals have access to the technology. You have the option of being able to see your subjects using this technology, which can better enable you to view their facial expressions and some body language. Like telephone interviews, this technology allows you to overcome geographic distance without the expense of travelling. However, unlike the telephone, which almost everyone understands how to use, VoIP can pose "technological" challenges for your subjects. It is important to ascertain whether or not your subjects are comfortable with the technology and can use the technology with ease. You do not want your precious interview time absorbed with overcoming technological glitches.

Virtual Reality. Virtual reality, such as Second Life and Active Worlds, are computer-simulated environments. Its use is becoming more common in education and research. There are ethical benefits to virtual reality and risky subjects can be researched. Virtual reality is cost effective and overcomes geographic distances. There is also the potential to have your subjects respond to scenarios, rather than use a question and answer interview format. It is anticipated that the use of virtual reality in research will continue to grow. Like VoIP, your subjects (and you) must be fairly tech-savvy to make use of this technology. If your subjects are not already using virtual reality it is not recommended that you conduct your interviews this way since there is a very steep learning curve.

Online Text. You can also conduct interviews using online text. In this case, you would have your subjects respond to written questions by typing a response. Because of the lack of voice and visual cues, this would most likely be a last resort for conducting a qualitative interview. This way of conducting an interview probably presents the biggest challenges for establishing rapport. If the subject is not already invested in the interview process at the start, he or she is less likely to become invested while texting as opposed to while engaging in a face-to-face conversation with you.

Interview Exercise

This exercise will focus on how to create a good interview schedule. Taking a topic of your choice, write 10–15 questions that you feel will elicit in-depth responses from your subjects. Follow these guidelines:

- Write open-ended questions; this encourages subjects to talk.
- Avoid "yes/no" questions.
- Avoid "why" questions.
- Avoid the use of jargon and academic terminology, unless it is appropriate for your subjects.

- Write your questions with language that will be clear to the subjects (questions asked of medical doctor should be worded very differently than questions asked of a former inmate).
- Write your questions using neutral language, avoiding bias, judgment or negative tone.
- Break compound questions into multiple questions.
- Ask questions about perspectives on facts, opinions/beliefs/values, feelings, sensory information, behaviors
- Begin with questions that will help build rapport, including general demographics.
- Place more sensitive questions toward the middle of the interview.
- Ask questions about the present first.
- Try to have a logical flow to your questions.
- Questions at the end of the interview should focus on summary, if appropriate.
- Include a final question that asks the subjects if they feel you've forgotten to ask about anything or if they would like to add something to their responses.

1. _____

_____

2. _____

_____

3. _____

_____

4. _____

_____

5. _____

_____

6. _____

_____

7. _____

_____

8. _____

_____

9. _____

_____

10. _____

_____

11. _____

_____

12. _____

_____

13. _____

_____

14. _____

_____

15. _____

_____

Now review your questions. Make sure that you have followed the guidelines closely. Practice your interview with a friend or relative and encourage that person to provide feedback to you. Do they understand the questions? Your subjects will be hearing your interview questions with fresh ears—so trying out your questions on them can be very beneficial.

Some subjects will be very verbose without much encouragement, while others are more tight-lipped. You need to be mindful about how open your subjects may be. Professionals like social workers tend to be very forthcoming in qualitative interviews, whereas teenage males tend to be much more close-mouthed. It is recommended that you create a few prompts for each question. For example:

1. "Can you tell me more about…"
2. "What do you mean by…"
3. "Can you give me an example?"
4. "You mentioned that…"
5. "What was it like…"

Remember not to overuse prompts and to vary them during the interview. They should be practiced along with the rest of the interview. You can also prompt respondents without using words by leaning forward, by silence, by a questioning look, by nodding, of by saying "hmmm." However, be wary of behavior that may discourage responses, such as jumping in to fill the silence too soon (give your subjects time to think and respond), appearing shocked at what a respondent has said, or suddenly scribbling notes.

Take a look at the sample demographics sheet and interview we have created below. The topic of this interview is "the experience of going away to college," and the subjects are traditional first-year college students (all subjects over 18, so they are not a protected population) who arrived on campus within the last two weeks. At the beginning of the interview, you will have your subjects fill out a short demographics sheet (which is included here first) and then the interview schedule.

Demographic Sheet

Name		Age	Gender
University		Major	
Days on Campus			

Interview Schedule

1. How did you come to the decision to go away to college, rather than attend a school close to home?
2. Tell me about your arrival here on campus.
    a. You mentioned _____ can you tell me more about that?
3. What has been the most surprising aspect of going away to college?
4. What is the best thing about going away to school?
5. What was the most challenging aspect of going away to college?
    a. How did you overcome that challenge?
6. What would you do differently if you had the whole experience to do over again?
7. What advice would you give to someone considering going away to school?
8. Is there anything else you would like to share with me about the experience of going away to college?

Conducting Your Field Test

Qualitative interviews require that a field test be conducted. The field test will enhance the credibility of your interview schedule. During the field test, you will submit your questions to a number of experts on your research topic, as well as one or more qualitative experts. (Be sure to check your school's requirements for the field test regarding the number and type of experts that need to be utilized.) Experts can be found at other universities, in professional organizations, even authors of journal articles may be willing to field test your interview schedule. These experts will provide you with academic feedback not limited to: wording of the questions, flow of the questions, appropriateness of the content area covered, and how well the questions will elicit good, qualitative responses.

Analysis of Interview Data

In almost all cases, you will want to begin analysis of your interview data after the first several interviews are completed. The first step is the transcription of the initial interviews and it is recommended that you transcribe your own data if possible as this will allow you to become immersed in the data in a way that simply reading the transcripts will not. The transcripts are reviewed not only to begin data analysis, but also to serve as a check on the interview process itself.

Beginning transcription as soon as possible allows you to double-check yourself as interviewer. You are able to see if you are making any glaring errors in your interviewing. (Are you talking too much? Too softly? Are you not pausing long enough to allow your subjects to really think about the questions before they answer?) You can also ascertain how the interviews themselves are going. (Are you obtaining the types of responses that you need and anticipated? Are there questions that are falling flat? Are your subjects answering you in one or two word responses?) If you discover that certain questions are not working in the context of the interview, you will want to edit them accordingly. You may find yourself eliminating some of your questions in favor of others. (Just make sure that you have written this type of editing into your IRB paperwork ahead of time so that you do not need to return to the IRB for another review.)

As you begin data analysis, you will want to being sorting your interview data into preliminary codes or themes. For each question—what do the subjects talk about? How do they respond? These are your first impressions of the data. As the interviews progress you will seek confirmation or disconfirmation of these initial impressions.

Bogan and Biklin (1998) recommend a process of first reviewing all of your transcripts, then going through initial coding and lastly a focused coding. The process of first reviewing all of the transcripts helps you to immerse yourself in the data and to get an overview of the material. The initial coding allows you to generate codes as they are suggested from the data. In the focused coding, you return to the initial coding and eliminate duplicate codes or combine codes that make sense. Bogan and Biklin (1998) recommend the following types of codes: setting, defining the situation, respondent perspective, respondents' ways of thinking about people or objects, process, activity, event, strategy, relationship/social structure, method. Of course, not all codes will work for all research and you will need to choose what makes sense for your study.

Miles and Huberman (1994) propose a three-step process for analysis consisting of data reduction, data display, and conclusion. Data reduction consists of making the initial selections about what is being researched. In this conceptualization of analysis, the analysis actually begins at the outset of planning the research. Data display attempts to find meaning in parts of the data using summaries or diagrams and charts. Finally, the conclusion compares, contrasts, and looks for patterns in the data.

Quotes are very important for qualitative studies. Quotes allow the subjects to "speak for themselves." While you may have often heard warnings about over-quoting in your writing, this is one place where you will not hear that admonishment. Quotes, in the presentation and analysis of qualitative interviews are not only good, but also absolutely necessary to allow the subjects to speak for themselves. You can use the words of your subjects to name themes and categories and you will use their words to convey the essence of meaning in your write-up.

Observation

Another method of data collection in qualitative research is observation, also referred to as field observations because they must be made in a naturalistic setting—in the field. This is a very important point because some novice researchers erroneously think that they can make observations during interview, but observations made during an interview are still interview data.

Observations can be undertaken for a variety of reasons in qualitative research. You can begin your study with observations to inform you of the nature of the field. If you are conducting observations in a work environment, you can observe your subjects as they go about their normal work routine. You can observe how individuals interact, how they communicate, and begin to make notes regarding what you observe, what it might mean, what you want to follow up on, and even begin your analysis.

Observation Exercise

One of the most common errors that are made when attempting to conduct qualitative observations is to fall back on our quantitative background and to rely upon counts or percentages. Qualitative observation is not about merely counting individuals or actions or categorizing, but about communicating descriptions. It is about giving both the researcher and the reader a feel for the field.

For this exercise, find a public place where you can observe people—a park or a mall food court—are excellent places to do this exercise. In the space provided below (or you may want to use your tablet or computer so that you can write as much as you like), begin with a full physical description of the scene. Be sure to include time of day. Include the five senses in your description. What are the smells? What does it sound like?

_____

_____

_____

_____

_____

_____

_____

_____

_____

Now review what you have written. Would it transport a reader to the spot where you are now? Have you clearly conveyed what is happening? If there are teenagers hanging out in the food court, did you describe what they are wearing? What their hair looks like? How they are interacting? Is there music playing? What are the food choices? Can you smell the pizza? The scene you are describing would be very different early in the morning when the mall walkers are out as opposed to six o'clock in the evening during the holiday season. In qualitative observations, you need to transport the reader to the scene that you are describing. It is almost a literary style of writing.

If you reread your field notes and you find that what you have recorded are the number of individuals who walked by you or that you counted the number of men and women or you counted interactions, without conveying the feeling of the scene, then you have falling into our quantitative way of life—which makes us very quantitative in nature. It is not uncommon during the first attempt at observations for novice researchers to fall back on this. Simply repeat the exercise, and this time do not allow yourself to count anything—but to describe everything.

Field Notes

Field notes allow the researcher to take comprehensive notes about a research setting. They are most commonly used in ethnography—although are very useful during all types of qualitative research both as a data point and as a tool for the researcher. Even the quantitative researcher can keep field notes about his or her research! When used as a data point, the notes that the researcher takes will be used in the analysis. If field notes are to be utilized in this manner, then there must be a clear plan at the outset of the research for both data collection and eventual data analysis. There are fewer worries when field notes are just a researcher's tool and not a data point. In this case, you can write anything and everything in your field notes and not worry about having useable data. You can record descriptions of people, places and events in your field notes. You can bring your own personal biases to the surface. You can mull over potential themes that you see, make notes for later follow up, and so forth.

Consider the following guidelines for writing field notes:

- Field notes should be taken either in the research setting or shortly after leaving the research setting. This is to preserve impressions as close to real-life as possible.
- Use whatever note-taking tool you are comfortable with from a small bound book, to a spiral notebook, to an electronic tablet. If it works well for you—that's what you should use.
- At the outset of each field notes session, make sure to note the time of day, date, and place of the notes. This can be very helpful if you are utilizing multiple sites in your research. It will also help you track events.
- Consider developing a coding system for different types of field notes so that they can be easily found during data analysis. Even if you are not utilizing the field notes as a data point, it can be very beneficial to review your field notes during the analysis process.
- Focus on writing a lot of description in your field notes. What does the scene look like? If there are interesting smells or tastes include those as well. Try to capture people's expressions. Include snippets of conversations. Think of the field notes almost as if you were writing a story—and tell that story!
- Do not shy away from self-reflection in your field notes. You will notice in the excerpt below the author (O'Reilly) expresses anxiety about the research—it is fine to do this. The way you feel about the research setting or in the research setting impact the research that you will do.
- Analysis can take place within the field notes as well.

Field Notes Example

The following is an excerpt of field notes from my own (O'Reilly) dissertation:

I was anxious over the past week about being here, researching here. I was especially nervous early this evening. I thought about not coming—but I had to. I arrived on time, at 9p.m. I met the charge nurse Janet (a pseudonym) who works 3-11. She is a middle-aged woman, slight of build, very nice and very helpful. She introduced me to some people and gave me some "info." Younger nurses here seem more "shell-shocked" by the ER space. She also said they've been really busy the past few weeks—and all of the residents are new. She admits, there's a lot of stress in the ER.

It was really busy. Janet got me into my first trauma—a woman who'd been in a motorcycle accident. She was only slightly injured. Shortly after, a very over-weight man in cardiac arrest came in. They were performing CPR, but soon they called it—just after 10p.m. This is the first person I've ever really seen die. Later, I went with one of the nurses and two guys down to the morgue. It seemed sad, yet so completely a part of being in the ER. No one else really took notice.

In this very brief excerpt (the field notes from that evening covered more than 10 pages in a steno pad), you will notice several important things. First, the time of arrival into the field is noted (the date was also noted at the beginning of the entry—which is not included in the excerpt). It is always a good idea to note particular fact, like the date and time. Weather might also be important. Second, there are brief descriptions of important individuals, like the charge nurse. When you are just entering the field, you cannot know for sure who will be important to your research and who won't be. It is a good idea to take down as much as possible without allowing your notes to become a distraction for you. Third, events were described, like the trauma and the death of the cardiac arrest. Fourth, the researchers feelings and reactions are noted. There are plenty of other possibilities for what can and should be included in your field notes. What is included is driven by the purpose of the research and what you, as a researcher, need from your field notes.

Field Notes Exercise

Taking good field notes can be a challenge for even a seasoned researcher. It is a good idea to practice in a setting that has less pressure than an actual research site. When I (O'Reilly) teach about qualitative, I often have my students conduct practice observations in a public setting. The exercise is as follows:

Choose a public setting like a coffee shop or a mall. Find a place to sit where you can also write in a notebook or on your laptop. Plan to spend at least twenty minutes observing. You will be recording three types of information in your field notes: background information, full descriptions, and analysis and self-reflection.

Background information that you record should include: time of day, place of observations, and a background of what usually happens at the site. This will "set the scene" for your observations.

Full descriptions include recording as many sensory impressions about the scene as you can. This will help you clearly recall the scene later. It will also allow you to use your observations during data analysis or the write-up of your research. You will want to record snippets of conversation. This also helps create a full picture of the setting and individuals within that setting.

Finally, use the field notes for self-reflection and analysis. You can jot down ideas as they occur to you for later follow-up. Write about how you personally react to the scene, especially if you find yourself reacting strongly. Record any biases and assumptions that you have about the setting. You can also record analyses of what is happening.

By the time twenty minutes are up, you should have at least five pages of notes—if not more. Now take some time to reread your field notes and reflect upon the process. Answer the following questions:

1. What was most difficult for you during the field notes exercise?_____

_____

_____

2. What was easiest about your field notes exercise?_____

_____

_____

3. What did you miss in your field notes?_____

_____

_____

Artifacts and Documents

Artifacts are objects and representations of a culture—the use of artifacts in research arose from anthropology but is now commonly found in qualitative research conducted in a wide variety of fields. A document used to be a written representation of an event or thoughts. Prior to the digital era, documents were written on paper but that is no longer the case. It should also be noted that there is some overlap between artifacts and documents—for example, a diary might be considered both an artifact and a document.

Artifacts commonly used in research encompass such diverse items as: art, photographs, videos, pottery, and diaries. There are wide-range of documents that may be used in research: state issued documents such as marriage licenses and death certificates, business issued documents, such as invoices and spreadsheets, and private documents, such as diaries and personal letters.

Documents can be utilized many ways within qualitative. A narrative analysis may be performed on the documents. The author (O'Reilly) once performed an analysis on personal letters that examined how the topic of love was juxtaposed with other topics within the letters. Documents can be used to clarify processes or procedures, for example when attempting to understand how a business or agency operates. Documents can be used simply to create a spreadsheet of ages (for example, the age at which juveniles commit their first crimes).

Artifacts, can be very useful in a qualitative study—even more so than documents. Photographs can be utilized to help a subject explain a particular time-period or event in his or her life. Diaries can be used and analyzed narratively, or entries can be used to describe events that have occurred. Subjects can also be asked to keep a diary during the study. Subjects can be asked to draw pictures or art they have created can be used in analysis.

Qualitative Methods Resources

Bogdan R. B., & Biklin, S. K. (1998). *Qualitative research for education: An introduction to theory and methods* (3rd ed.). Needham Heights, MA: Allyn and Bacon.

Emerson, R. M., Fretz, R. I. & Shaw, L. L. (1995). *Writing ethnographic fieldnotes*. Chicago: University of Chicago Press.

Kawulich, B. B. (2005). Participant observation as a data collection method. *Forum Qualitative Sozialforschung/Forum: Qualitative Social Research,* 6(2), Art. 43. Retrieved from http://www.qualitative-research.net/index.php/fqs/article/view/466/996

Kivits, J. (2005). Online interviewing and the research relationship. In C.Hine (Ed.), *Virtual methods: Issues in social research on the Internet* (pp.35-50). Oxford: Berg.

Kvale, S. (1983). The qualitative research interview: A phenomenological and a hermeneutical mode of understanding. *Journal of Phenomenological Psychology, 14*, 171-196.

Markham, A. M. (2004). The Internet as research context. In C. Seale, G. Gobo, J. Gubrium, & D. Silverman (Eds.), *Qualitative research practice* (pp.358-374). London: Sage.

Marshall, C., & Rossman, G. B. (1989). *Designing qualitative research*. Newbury Park, CA: Sage.

Miles, M. B., & Huberman, A. M. (1994). Qualitative data analysis: An expanded sourcebook. Thousand Oaks, CA: Sage Publications.

Rubin, H. J. & Rubin, I.S. (2005). *Qualitative interviewing: The art of hearing da*ta. Thousand Oaks, CA: Sage Publications

Steinar, K. (1996). *InterViews: An introduction to qualitative interviewing*. Thousand Oaks, CA: Sage Publications

Turner, D. W. (2010). Qualitative Interview Design: A Practical Guide for Novice Investigators. *The Qualitative Report,15*, 754-760.

Chapter Ten – The Challenges of Qualitative

Qualitative research presents even the seasoned researcher with many challenges. There are challenges to your research skill set and there are ethical challenges. There are feasibility issues that exist in qualitative that do not exist in quantitative. And there are plenty of potential stumbling blocks in the qualitative research process.

Ethical Issues and the Institutional Review Board

There are ethical considerations that must be addressed in regard to any research study, but many of these are more prominent within qualitative research because of the interaction that the researcher will have with the subjects. Ethical considerations can arise from:

- The category of subjects in the study—especially if they are from a vulnerable population (like minors).
- The type of information or data that is being sought from the subjects (for example, information about sensitive issues like abuse).
- Who the researcher is in relation to the subjects (for example, if there is a prior relationship between researcher and subject, especially if that relationship is one in which the researcher has a more powerful position than the subject—such as: doctor-patient, therapist-client, employee-supervisor).
- The identity of the researcher—particularly if the researcher has a vested interest in the outcome of the study, or is collecting data from his or her own workplace.

Preparing for the Institutional Review Board

Institutional Review Boards (IRBs) are federally mandated to oversee research and protect human subjects. IRBs are in place at universities and other organizations, such as hospitals. There are also privately run IRBs. Your university's IRB will look at your research proposal to ensure that it will not cause harm to your subjects, in particular, or to any class of individuals, in general. The IRB also serves to protect you, as the researcher, both legally and physically, and also to protect the university, legally.

While many students see the IRB as a potential stumbling block, in actuality, they can be a considerable help to any researcher. Visit your school's IRB webpage early on in your research process. You are likely to find useful forms, submission dates, and information. You can contact your institution's IRB early in the process via e-mail or phone to ask specific questions pertaining to your research.

The IRB is made up of a committee of individuals. Many of the individuals will have a background in science, however, all IRBs must also have at least one person who is a non-scientist community representative. If an IRB will review research dealing with vulnerable populations, there must be an individual who can serve as a representative for those individuals who is a part of that IRB. For example, if your research deals with children, one of the people who review your research proposal will have specialized experience working with children.

The best way to get through the IRB is to give serious consideration to the possible ethical issues that might be contained within your research. In particular, you need to consider ethical issues from a research standpoint. For example, individuals who work with prisoners on a daily basis often do not consider them to be "vulnerable," but as far as research is concerned, they are.

Qualitative research, since it generally involves significant contact with subjects and often consists of long-interviews, which could contain material that is disturbing to subjects, will receive special consideration. Consider the following questions:

- ***Is there benefit in your research?***
    - o All IRBs will look at a potential study to make sure that there is scientific merit to the study: that it—at least in some small way—advances the discipline, and that it is a well-crafted study.
    - o If your study is low-risk, there does not need to be a significant benefit; however, if you have a higher level of risk in your study, then there correspondingly must also be greater benefit.
    - o Generally speaking, social science dissertations must be low-risk because they are low-benefit. Do not overestimate the potential benefit of your study.
- ***Is there the potential for harm in your research?***
    - o The IRB will look for the potential of physical harm to you or to your subjects. For example, if you wanted to go to offenders' homes to collect data, the IRB would very likely consider that to be too much of a risk to your safety to approve.
    - o The IRB will also look for the potential of psychological or emotional harm to potential research subjects—which is the most common factor for concern in studies. It is unlikely that an IRB will allow a dissertation-level researcher to work with subjects who are likely to be harmed (for example, individuals who have been victims of violent crimes, individuals with post traumatic stress disorder, individuals who have attempted suicide), unless you have special training or experience, and if you put into place special precautions to guard against harm.
    - o The potential for psychological harm is of particular concern in qualitative research. Your interview schedule will be especially scrutinized.
- ***Does your research deal with subjects who are vulnerable?***
    Ethical concerns in research studies can revolve around the subjects if the subjects are from a vulnerable population (for example, children, prisoners, cognitively impaired individuals). It can be difficult to collect primary data from vulnerable populations and any study that proposes to do so will receive extra scrutiny and, most likely, a full IRB review.
    Because there is so much contact with subjects in qualitative research, vulnerability becomes a special concern.
- ***Are you dealing with a sensitive subject matter?*** Sensitive subjects can range from suicide, to mental health issues, to post traumatic stress, to sexual behavior. In qualitative, the long-interview will often ask for experience and details of what

happened. It can be very traumatic for an individual to discuss a past sexual assault or the experience of living with an alcoholic parent.

- ***Is it obvious that certain individuals or sites are being used in your research?*** It is important that the identities of your research subjects and research sites remain anonymous and that they cannot be associated with particular statistics/statements/opinions in your published dissertation. Make sure no one and no site can be identified or gleaned from what you have written.
- ***Are you somehow involved in a dual relationship with your subjects?*** Dual relationships are not allowed between researcher and subject, primarily because of the potential for coercion and bias. Dual relationships may arise between teacher-student, therapist-client, doctor-patient and so forth. If the researcher is in the dominant position over the potential subject, then coercion may be present. If the researcher is using his or her own clients for research, the researcher has a vested interest in the outcome of the study. IRBs also are reluctant to allow researchers to collect data where they work.
- ***Does the possibility for coercion exist in your study?*** The IRB will look for the possibility of coercion in your study. The IRB will also look at whether or not the remuneration offered in the study could be coercive. For a poor or homeless individual, ten dollars might be considered coercive, whereas for a mid-level executive, $100 would not be considered coercive.
- ***Are you utilizing secondary data for your study?*** The utilization of secondary data will circumvent many IRB issues. These studies generally qualify for an exempt review. Since you will not be interacting with subjects, the study is deemed to be low-risk. You are also able to utilize secondary data from vulnerable populations—which may be the only way for you to conduct research with these populations. No consent materials will be required. The IRB will be interested in whether or not you can obtain access to the data, and it will still look at the scientific merit of the study. However, within qualitative research there are far fewer opportunities for utilizing secondary data than in quantitative studies. However, it is not impossible. Secondary data may be in the form of diaries kept in the past, or newspaper articles or other artifacts and trace evidence created by humans.

Feasibility Issues

Feasibility must be considered in any research study. Feasibility examines how easy, or difficult, it will be to complete a study. Feasibility issues can arise at all junctures of research—from the selection of the topic to data collection—and it is not so much of a matter of whether or not the study is an interesting idea or addresses a gap in the literature—but whether the study can *actually* be carried out in a timely and cost-effective manner. The following are some critical junctures at which issues of feasibility can crop up:

- Study is too broad in scope: would require a multitude of data types to carry out or is really a broad social problem rather than a research problem
- Study will take too long to carry out
- Subjects will be difficult to locate or may not readily participate in research
- Subjects are members of a protected and/or vulnerable population
- Topic deals with immoral, illegal, or unusual activities and subjects may be unwilling to discuss them

- The topic of the dissertation is a topic that subjects are unlikely to participate in because of the personal nature of what is being asked
- Research might harm the subjects—either physically or psychologically
- The study is more than minimal risk but does not offer more than minimal benefit, so the IRB is unlikely to approve
- The research questions will be difficult to answer because they are too broad, too vague, or are ill-defined
- The study will require considerable funds to carry out, and the dissertation is unfunded and you do not have the extra cash to put into the study
- Permission from a specific site is required and that site is unlikely to provide permission, for example, schools, police departments, prisons
- Permission will be required from multiple sites

Stumbling Blocks During Qualitative Research

We all encounter stumbling blocks during research and qualitative research is especially prone to stumbling blocks. This may be because of the complexity of qualitative research and the skill it takes to conduct qualitative research well. As soon as you come across a stumbling block, you must devise a plan of attack, and overcome it.

Qualitative research process in general. Perhaps the most commonly encountered stumbling block encountered while conducting qualitative research for the novice qualitative researcher is the mystique that surrounds qualitative research in general. Unlike quantitative where everything is about the numbers and the statistic that you perform, analyzing verbal data (as most qualitative research consists of) is much more difficult. The key to not letting the qualitative research process itself become a stumbling block is to become as familiar as you can with that process—know it forward and backwards. Read about it—as much as you can. Start with this text—and continue from there. There is nothing mystical about qualitative. Regardless of which qualitative approach you are using for your study, plan your research exactly as you would plan to make a gourmet meal—leave nothing to chance. Every step that you take in your research should be crystal clear to you and written down in your write-up—just like a recipe in a cookbook. Qualitative research does not mean that research is sloppy or vague.

Subject recruitment. Even though qualitative studies require far fewer subjects than a quantitative study (a quantitative study might require hundreds of subjects versus a qualitative study that might require 15), subject recruitment is still a considerable challenge. Subject recruitment in qualitative may be difficult because of the time commitment required from the subjects to participate in the research. Subject recruitment may be difficult because of who the subjects are—they may be members of a protected population. Subject recruitment may be difficult just because many people simply are not interested in participating in research.

In quantitative, it is not uncommon for the data collection time commitment from subjects to be under 30 minutes, but the long interviews required in qualitative often require a time-commitment of 45-60 minutes minimum and in some cases there may be multiple interviews required. This is a considerable time commitment for someone who is very busy—or for anyone. If you are interested in interviewing doctors or CEOs, chances are they will not have the spare time to devote to being in your study.

If your subjects are members of a protected population (individuals under the control of the criminal justice system, children, individuals with cognitive deficits) the Institutional

Review Board may be reluctant to grant permission to you to allow interviews. In qualitative, there is more contact with subjects than in quantitative. (Qualitative generally conducts long interviews—of anywhere from 45 minutes to an hour in length; while quantitative administers normed, validated measures—which often take 30 minutes or less.) Almost any time members of a protected population are subjects in a study; the IRB will conduct a full review of the study, which will take more time than an exempt review or an expedited review. You may need to incorporate additional protections for your subjects before you receive IRB approval, which adds design challenges to your study.

You also need to deal with the fact that, in general, people will not be eager to participate in your study. You should always have at least one back up plan for subject recruitment ready to go if your first recruitment attempt is unsuccessful. Think about where you can find subjects. If you want to recruit former steelworkers—where would you find them? Is there a bar where they still gather? If so, you could post a call for subjects there or even approach individuals personally. Is it possible to get a list of former union members? You might be able to send letters to the members. Do they still live in the area around the mill? You could recruit by sending out a mailing, or by posting a call for subjects in a community center.

Site permission. A novice qualitative researcher might believe that it can be much easier to recruit subject from an agency. If you are interested in social workers who work with children in the foster care system, you might consider recruiting them from the agency for which they work—however, this is often a mistake; most agencies are far less than eager to have researchers interviewing their employees and obtaining site permission can actually be much more difficult than recruiting your subjects as individuals. If your research centers on a particular site, then that site not allowing you to recruit can be devastating. If your potential subjects are middle school teachers, rather than try to access them through a particular school district, access them through a professional organization for teachers. In this way, the agency no longer acts as a gatekeeper—but you are still able to access individuals for your research.

Qualitative interview problems. In most qualitative research, everything centers upon the interview process and the rich verbal data that you get from the interviews. Qualitative interviewing is a skill—and it can prove a difficult skill to acquire without practice. If you are not getting rich data during your interviews, then your analysis may become seriously compromised because there will literally be very little to analyze.

There are two approaches that will help you assure that your interviews are good qualitative interviews and you obtain the type of rich data that is required for your research. First, begin by practicing your interviews with a family member or friend. This will allow you to obtain feedback from an individual who can listen to your questions with fresh ears. Earlier in the text, we completed an exercise on composing your interview. The feedback that you receive on your interview skills should focus more on *how* you conduct your interview. Are you asking questions too fast or slow? Are you talking too much? Taking too many notes? Making your "participant" feel judged?

A beneficial way to make sure that you are obtaining rich interview data is to utilize a form of triangulation for your interview data—have another individual listen to your interviews and offer feedback. If you are a student, this can be your chair or mentor. You can also consider pairing with a more experienced qualitative researcher and having this person provide feedback on your interviews.

Let your dissertation chair listen to your interview tapes or read your transcripts. If your chair checks your interviews early on—for example, after the first two or three interviews— interview problems can be caught early and corrected. Your chair can make specific recommendations to obtain more robust interviews—some of which may include reworking your questions, or practicing more listening in your interviews.

Qualitative saturation problems. Qualitative interviews are generally conducted until saturation is reached—which means that new subjects are repeating what previous subjects have already told us. Problems can occur when saturation is reached too early in the interview process or when it is not reached at all.

If saturation is reached too early you may be left with too little data to analyze. This can indicate that your topic of choice perhaps should have been explored quantitatively rather than qualitatively, or that the interview was too narrow in focus. Because qualitative relies on the richness of your data, this must be addressed for the study to truly be a success. This can be remedied by adjusting the qualitative approach used for the research—for example, moving from a phenomenological study to a case study and incorporate other data points. You could also adjust your interview schedule and interview more subjects. You can even build this type of adjustment into your research at the beginning by conducting tiered interviews.

On the other hand, we may fail to reach saturation—and not know if we have thoroughly explored our topic; in this case, we may want to continue interviewing. This can also mean that our chosen topic is too broad and we may need to narrow our focus.

Qualitative data not rich enough. In qualitative research, stumbling blocks commonly arise when the data is not rich enough for analysis. If your interviews are not yielding rich data, then you may need to revisit your interview questions and edit them so that they elicit fuller responses from the subjects. In some cases—in qualitative—when you were going to review existing documents, those documents may not be as fruitful as you originally thought they would be. In that case, you need to present what you can from that data and hopefully there are enough other data points in your study to make up for lack in one type of data. This can be particularly tricky, and is one of the key reasons why we spend so much time preparing the design phase of a qualitative study.

Is the problem the interview questions? Is the problem that the subjects do not want to spend the time giving you the rich data? Are the subjects the type who don't like to talk much—like teenage boys? Are you interviewing people who are under time pressure? Are your subjects reluctant to talk at work?

Writing. Writing often poses a stumbling block for students in dissertation. Even for a solid writer—who has written or even published academic papers—writing a full book (which is what the dissertation is) can be very challenging. After reading this text, you should be able to break your writing down into smaller pieces, which will make the task more manageable. For students who are poor writers or who lack the foundation of good grammar, usage, and mechanics, the writing of the dissertation poses a much greater problem. It is very important that you use whatever tools your university has provided to obtain an honest and critical assessment of your writing (remember what I said earlier about accepting feedback and criticism), and then to use that assessment to improve your writing. It can be very beneficial to take a technical writing class. There really is no other way to improve your writing than to write.

The important take-away is that there are many potential stumbling blocks in conducting a qualitative study. You, as a qualitative researcher must be aware of these stumbling blocks and strive to address them as you design your study—well before you ever begin to collect any data or have contact with your first subject.

APPENDIX – Tricks from the Library

While there are many tricks you may learn from your librarian, I've selected some of my own favorites to include here:

Seminal Works. In order to do any literature review properly, you must know what the seminal works are in your topic or discipline. Seminal works are very important pieces of literature that have changed the discipline or moved the discipline forward in very important ways. They will be frequently cited in other literature in your discipline. Make sure you know the seminal works in your topic area and always use them to place your dissertation work in the context of the broader literature.

Bibliography Mining and Cited Reference Searching. Bibliographic mining and cited reference searching are related techniques. You begin with a really great article and from that article you review all of the articles that it cites in its reference section. Then, you take that really great article and find articles that have been published more recently than it which cite it as a source. This helps you to see an arc of the literature and can be a great way to find many articles related to your topic (and also many authors who do work in your topic area).

Reference or Citation Management Software. These software tools are a great way to organize your references for your dissertation or for any other academic writing you are doing. Once you put your references into the software you can use them over and over for any writing that you do which utilizes the same articles. It makes it a lot easier than having to re-create your reference list each time you write a paper or an article.

Author and Journal Notifications. Many academic libraries offer you the service of receiving author and journal notifications as long as you are a registered student. To set up journal notifications, let the librarian know what journals you are interested in (and there should be several), and you will receive an e-mail notification with a link to the journal every time a new issue becomes available. Author notifications are similar; you will be notified every time important authors to your dissertation publish something new.

Appendix – Qualitative Journals

American Anthropologist (American Anthropological Association)

American Ethnologist (American Ethnological Association)

Anthropology Today (Royal Anthropological Institute of Great Britain and Ireland)

Ethnography

Field Methods (formerly Cultural Anthropology Methods)

Forum: Qualitative Sozialforschung / Forum: Qualitative Social Research [online]

Gestalt Theory: An International Multidisciplinary Journal

The Grounded Theory Review: An International Journal

International Journal of Qualitative Methods (International Institute for Qualitative Methodology, University of Alberta)

International Journal of Qualitative Studies in Education

International Journal of Social Research Methodology

Journal of Contemporary Ethnography

Journal of Phenomenological Psychology

Journal of the British Society for Phenomenology

Narrative Inquiry

Phenomenological Inquiry (World Institute for Advanced Phenomenological Research and Learning)

Qualitative Health Research

Qualitative Inquiry

Qualitative Market Research: An International Journal

The Qualitative Report (Nova Southeastern University--School of Social and Systemic Studies) [online]

Qualitative Research

Qualitative Research in Psychology

Qualitative Research Journal (Association for Qualitative Research)

Qualitative Social Work

Qualitative Sociology

Quality & Quantity: International Journal of Methodology

Recherches Qualitatives (Association pour la Recherche Qualitative (ARQ)) [online]

Research & Theory (National Council on Family Relations)

Resources for Feminist Research / Documentation sur la Recherche Feministe Symbolic Interaction (Society for the Study of Symbolic Interaction)

Systemic Practice and Action Research

TAMARA: Journal for Critical Oganization Inquiry

Theory and Research in Social Education (National Council for the Social Studies)